SIX DAYS OF IMPOSSIBLE

NAVY SEAL
HELL WEEK

A DOCTOR LOOKS BACK

R O B E R T
A D A M S

 FriesenPress

Suite 300 - 990 Fort St
Victoria, BC, V8V 3K2
Canada

www.friesenpress.com

ISBN
978-1-5255-0443-3 (Hardcover)
978-1-5255-0444-0(Paperback)
978-1-5255-0445-7 (eBook)

1. Biography & Autobiography, Military

Distributed to the trade by The Ingram Book Company

Table of Contents

Prologue

NAVY SEAL CODE

In times of war or uncertainty there is a special breed of warrior ready to answer our Nation's call. A common man with uncommon desire to succeed.

Forged by adversity, he stands alongside America's finest special operations forces to serve his country and the American people, and to protect their way of life.

I am that man.

My Trident is a symbol of honor and heritage. Bestowed upon me by the heroes that have gone before, it embodies the trust of those whom I have sworn to protect. By wearing the Trident, I accept the responsibility of my chosen profession and way of life. It is a privilege that I must earn every day.

My loyalty to Country and Team is beyond reproach. I humbly serve as a guardian to my fellow Americans, always ready to defend those who are unable to defend themselves. I do not advertise the nature of my work, nor seek recognition for my actions. I voluntarily accept the inherent hazards of my profession, placing the welfare and security of others before my own.

I serve with honor on and off the battlefield. The ability to control my emotions and my actions, regardless of circumstance, sets me apart from other men.

Uncompromising integrity is my standard. My character and honor are steadfast. My word is my bond.

We expect to lead and be led. In the absence of orders, I will take charge, lead my teammates, and accomplish the mission. I lead by example in all situations.

I will never quit. I persevere and thrive on adversity. My Nation expects me to be physically harder and mentally stronger than my enemies. If knocked down, I will get back up, every time. I will draw on every remaining ounce of strength to protect my teammates and to accomplish our mission. I am never out of the fight.

We demand discipline. We expect innovation. The lives of my team-mates and the success of our mission depend on me – my technical skill, tactical proficiency, and attention to detail. My training is never complete.

We train for war and fight to win. I stand ready to bring the full spectrum of combat power to bear in order to achieve my mission and the goals established by my country. The execution of my duties will be swift and violent when required, yet guided by the very principles that I serve to defend.

Brave men have fought and died building the proud tradition and feared reputation that I am bound to uphold. In the worst of condi-tions, the legacy of my teammates steadies my resolve and silently guides my every deed.

I will not fail.

The Navy SEAL Code suggests that there is, absolutely, a reason for Hell Week. It states, "I will never quit" and it ends with "I will not fail."

Most books and stories written by – or about – SEALs comment on their own personal Hell Week. It is a unique event in the world of military training, which binds those that complete this task together. Every BUD/S (Basic Underwater Demolition/SEAL) graduate has completed this individual test of will early in his training and has thus accomplished both the improbable and the unimaginable.

If you have not done it, you can only try to imagine it, and your imagination will fail you.

For those who have completed Hell Week, few can effectively describe the difficulty, pain, bone-shattering rigors, numbing cold, and prolonged, but endured, suffering. There is a real, and much anticipated, elation that follows winning the battle with one's self, and this joy is uplifting and personal. No medical or psychological study, so far, has been able to predict who will succeed or fail. It is an individual test, set against multiple personal motivations, that must be played out as part of a singular and team effort. It is undeniably one of the most difficult military endurance tests known.

As a physician now, I followed the writings of other SEALs in hopes of finding an effective description of our shared experiences. Most writers discover the same issue that I have found. There are not enough descriptive words to effectively describe the event. There has never been anything else quite like it. The closest missive that I have found to help understand something like Hell Week was written by another physician and psychiatrist after he survived the Jewish prison camps of World War II Germany. *Man's Search for Meaning* by Victor E. Frankl is an enduring work that examines Nazi death camp survivors. He points out that the pursuit of meaning, not pleasure, is our life's driving force.

> "When a man finds that it is his destiny to suffer, he must accept his suffering as his task; his single and unique task. He will have to acknowledge the fact that even in suffering he is unique and alone in the universe. No one can relieve him of his suffering or suffer in his place. His unique opportunity lies in the way in which he bears his burden."

> —Dr. Viktor Frankl, *Man's Search for Meaning.*

I will record the following events as reported by the eleven men in our class that completed Hell Week and graduated. Eight of us had careers that spanned over forty years in almost every UDT or SEAL Team. In interviewing my classmates, I tried to hear their stories as an analyst with a medical background, looking for something in common that we all may have shared or done or learned that contributed to our being able to complete Hell Week. I did discover a common thread.

Our combined recollections will report on those six days of life-altering time. It will look at the thoughts and actions that arose from a test that challenges imagination; it will tell of *our* Hell Week, one made up of men just like the ones today. More than 320 classes have completed Hell Week since the formation of the SEAL Teams in 1962, but the total percentage of graduates from each class remains very small.

This missive is told from the remembered past with a nod to the current time. The eleven men that graduated (and five corpsmen who joined our class after Hell Week for Phase 2 and 3 training) are brothers still. Few men or women will ever know the bond that is created by those shared experiences. Some of our wives, in the past, have expressed jealousy over this bond.

"I will never be as close to my husband as you were then; and maybe still are. Of that one reality, I will always be jealous of you," one wife shared.

Interestingly, this incredibly difficult week of individual and group trials has not changed much over time. It remains almost identical in design and function. It still takes an individual to a point of absolute physical exhaustion and mental disbelief. When he reaches his expected point of total exhaustion, he will discover (as all graduates have before him) that there is a place in his mind that must be discovered, examined quickly, and mastered. The body will stop at some point, physically and metabolically, but unless those two events occur at the same time, the mind can push us much, much, further.

The main purpose of this week is to help each person discover that the actual limits of human endurance are defined primarily by the individual.

The men in the following pages are real. Their stories are as accurate as I can make them. In some cases, the men and their stories represent composite men or events created for helping better understand the actions and thoughts of men forging on through situations that are easier described than understood.

The present-day "tadpoles" (SEAL trainees) are no different than those that have gone before, and they are still lining up daily on the famed asphalt "grinder" to see if they can make it one more day, or one more hour. The "grinder" is a term given to the rock-hard black asphalt area that is surrounded by the U-shaped sections of the training area. It is shielded from view and open to the weather. There is a raised wooden platform at the open end of the U that faces the windowed rooms containing the officers and staff that monitor all aspects of performance and training. Next to the wooden platform is a bathtub filled with water for use by the instructors when encouragement is needed. This area is half the size of a football field and has bright yellow swim fins painted every few feet to mark where the trainees will stand in formation, facing the platform, backs to the windows, while lining up for daily physical training events.

The challenges are no fewer and no greater. But the missions that await them are much more demanding. Our nation needs them in often unnamed places today, and in dark, hostile, yet-to-be identified places tomorrow.

There are two differences that deserve comment. There is more emphasis on identifying and rewarding positive effort. In the past, emphasis on negative performance may have pushed the potential graduate over the line too soon. This would be especially true in the later stages of Hell Week, when defenses were low. And the training is more scientifically monitored and managed. Safety and health is more closely managed. The need for SEAL warriors has never been greater than it is today. The Naval Special Warfare training community cannot afford to lose a future warrior due to an avoidable injury.

Few will try, and even fewer will succeed. By the end of this narrative, you may appreciate why.

Surprisingly, and this is a recent phenomenon, a rare few will make it all the way to the end of Hell Week, and six months of training, complete an entire year of additional required training, only to decide they do not want the life of combat they have trained for. They just wanted to take the test. These few will be released from service and likely go on to other successes in life. They will never become warriors, and they will never defend America with their lives.

Sleep well at night, for others stand ready, now as before, to protect and defend the freedoms we all enjoy.

Hooyah!

SIX DAYS OF IMPOSSIBLE

Fitness and physical prowess counts to a significant degree, but in those telling moments in Hell Week, it is, without question, a trainees' heart and soul's resolve that will make or break him. When a trainee has not slept for 48-60 hours and the cold has essentially taken over his brain, the "frog brain," or that internal fire, is what keeps survivors moving minute by tortuous minute to that final hour when they are secured from Hell Week. This book truly captures the essence of Hell Week.

—CDR (SEAL) Steve Frisk
BUD/S instructor for 19 BUD/S classes

"Courage is not having the strength to go on;
it is going on when you don't have the strength."
—Theodore Roosevelt

Chapter 1

The cold of winter – somewhere in Hell Week

The warm urine running down Ensign Randy Albracht's left leg felt wonderful. It pooled in his boot as he shifted position to allow more warmth to run down his other leg. The incessant shivering continued, and he paused to wonder briefly if urine in his boots could somehow cause harm. It did not matter. Warmth mattered. He had just completed the run from the mess hall back to the BUD/S training area beach, and the "down boats" order gave his neck and back a break as they all watched the crashing surf ahead. He still had to keep swallowing to hold breakfast down, where he desperately needed it, but now was the time to get rid of the unnecessary fluid from his coffee, hot chocolate, and Pepsi he had drank with his enormous breakfast.

He was not alone, as he and others briefly paused to enjoy moments of warm liquid filling their boots. There had been time at the mess hall to visit the bathroom, and some did, but it interfered with the eating time. Physiologic needs hit all trainees at about the same time. Little did they know, as they used their internal warmth to ease icy skin discomfort, they were also *sacrificing* stored body heat. Their core body temperatures were dropping. Without constant movement and calories, hypothermia would take over, and brain functions would worsen beyond its currently degraded state. Everyone would echo the thought that if drinking cobra venom would help them now, they would all gladly drink it.

ENS Albracht was fit and confident, and he came to training originally from Iowa. He had a wrestler's body with wide shoulders and a muscularly thin waist. His black hair was thick, and his beard was dark, and with his shirt off, he reminded some of a gorilla. He had hair everywhere. There was no body fat visible. He was strong as an ox and had the defined muscles to prove it. He could swim well, but he had never swum with swim fins. This would later prove to be a problem.

Randy had begun his military training in Army ROTC, but he had wangled a Navy appointment on graduation to become a pilot. During his flight training in Pensacola, Florida, he was told he would have to fly the back seat as a flight navigator. This was not what he wanted. He had asked about other service options and, while reviewing them, was told that the SEALs "worked out a lot."

As a collegiate wrestler, that sounded just fine, so without much additional information, he requested BUD/S. This course change brought his tanned, fit, muscular body to Coronado. He had no idea what was ahead. It was just another adventure in a life planned for adventure.

Now he was as cold as an Iowa winter in the snow had ever made him. He oversaw a boat crew of shivering sailors and faced an ocean of frothy white crashing waves that scared the last bit of piss out of him.

He was confident of his future success, but a question lingered. Could he master swimming with fins? He was doing poorly on the one-mile swims with fins. He had only once made a passing time, and *that* had occurred with some unseen help. Seaman Don Sayre was the best fin swimmer in the class, so on the last one-mile night swim test, he had deliberately teamed with Randy. Each swim pair was joined at the waist by a rope. This was operationally appropriate, and a safety measure. But this time, to help, Randy was instructed to roll on his back and kick with his fins as Don pulled with all his might to get them both across the finish line on time. It worked. The instructors did not see the subterfuge, but they did note that Sayre was not the first to finish for a change.

There were seventy men in the class when it started. The Naval Special Warfare Center training facility was (and is) tucked away discretely on the

Pacific shore of the expensive Silver Strand in Coronado, California. High rise condominiums dotted the beach, and world-class hotels drew tourists to a lovely beach sometimes abused by loudly singing Navy men wrapped in heavy orange kapok lifejackets and running with rubber boats on their heads. This was just part of their training conducted south of these high-rises.

Eight naval officers and sixty-two Navy enlisted men from all over the country, with various ranks and specialty ratings, had made up the initial gathering of trainees. Some had no idea what they were doing there; others were convinced they knew just what was ahead. Some were great swimmers, some were great runners, and some had barely been challenged in the past by sports or personal exertions. Everyone had passed the required physical fitness test with running, swimming, push-ups, sit-ups, pull-ups, and flutter kicks.

The screening test was not very difficult for most men with a sports background. It tested for minimum competency in the basic physical skills necessary to survive the most difficult military training in the world. A great score on the test did help with the selection process. They would begin as human clay to be squished and molded into an expected, well-defined, clearly-tested end state. Everyone would graduate as almost Olympic capable athletes, able to continue the with twelve more months of advanced training needed to operate in combat alongside the instructors who watched and groomed them. The would be awarded their "Budweiser" SEAL insignia after completing this additional training.

ENS Albracht had learned, after volunteering to go, that BUD/S was an acronym for Basic Underwater Demolition/SEAL. SEAL is an acronym for Sea, Air, Land, the three environments they are required to master. There was one SEAL Team, one Swimmer Delivery Vehicle (SDV) Team, and two Underwater Demolition Teams (UDT) assigned to operate on each coast of the United States when his class started. They were commanded by a Naval Special Warfare Group staff at each location in Coronado, California, and Little Creek, Virginia

Shivering right next to him was his current swim buddy and the class leading petty officer, PN2 Mike Suter. He was a "rollback" from a previous class. He was tall, handsome, tanned, and muscularly thin with a hard, acne-scarred face and focused glare. He was the only smoker in the class when it started and was proud that he had always smoked only Marlboro reds. But he had finally quit smoking as the weeks leading up to his second Hell Week got harder. He had failed one of his earlier qualifying swim tests a few times, which would normally be too much to ignore, but the instructors and his classmates liked him so much they rolled him back to this class, which gave him time to practice swimming techniques and get his times better.

This was not a good weakness for a future frogman. He and the instructors all knew that this was going to be his last chance, for he had been a medical drop from an earlier East Coast training class, due to frostbite earned on his first night of the previous winter Hell Week. His past Hell Week had been the last time training had been held in Little Creek, Virginia. Now it was all centralized only in Coronado, California, and Class 81 was his last chance at a future in the Teams. He was very leery of the cold, and he had his bare wet hands tucked under his armpits with the paddle cradled in the crook of his arm. He watched the surf with a detached calm.

He had waited three and a half years for this chance to try again and had made this last-chance assignment a condition of his Navy reenlistment. It had been written into his reenlistment contract, which was a guarantee he had learned to ask for while working as a personnel petty officer in the ship's administrative office. This office processed all orders and reenlistments on his ship. He was ready now, and he was not planning to fail again. The irony, which struck at his core, was that he had carefully planned to start in a summer class. Now, due to the swimming issue and class rollback, he found himself facing another Hell Week in winter. His fingers throbbed.

Was there no justice in this world? Mike thought to himself again. He knew that a recurrent hypothermia injury was much more likely in someone that had suffered it previously. But it did not matter to him either then or now. Whatever it took, he would complete the tasks, frostbite or not. He was made of the right stuff. He knew it, and the instructors strongly suspected it. Time would tell. He was fully prepared to lose a finger or endure a life-altering injury if it allowed him to make it to the Teams. Everyone often said stuff like that. He meant it in every fiber of his body.

"Up boats," came the order, and each crew groaned together as they hoisted their rubber boats back onto their aching heads, necks, and shoulders.

"Success is stumbling from failure to failure
with no loss of enthusiasm."
—Winston S. Churchill

Chapter 2
Getting ready – high school, age 16

The black and white striped sheepshead fish swam lazily around the railroad trestle piling as I aimed my homemade Hawaiian sling spear at its eyes. I was six feet deep, in calm brackish water, with fins moving me quietly closer. The mask was starting to fog up. The spear's elastic band was cut from old bicycle inner tubes and nailed to my broomstick spear. They cut into my sixteen-year-old hands as I lined up the shot. I was excited. With accuracy learned from many afternoons of snorkeling around these Pensacola, Florida, waters, the broomstick, armed with trident-shaped barbed tips, shot forward and buried itself into the fish's side with a pleasing *klunk*. It wriggled the paralyzed dance of death as I solemnly celebrated the kill. I would cook it for dinner tonight to go with whatever mom had chosen for us. She was used to my water oriented independence. I was a junior in high school, played tuba in the marching band, and was only sure of one thing. I would never join the military as four generations of family men before me had done. However, I had no other goal in mind, except college and girls.

Later that afternoon, in my room off the garage, in Quarters 22, across from the football field where LT Roger Staubach, USN, led his semi-pro football team to victory each football season, I lay on my pull-out couch bed and read the June 1967 issue of *Reader's Digest*. While flipping to the jokes section, my eye caught the page 49 story titled "Super commandos of the Wetlands."

"A small elite unit of the U.S. Navy, whose extraordinary exploits were secret until recently, has proved, in the jungles of Vietnam, to be perhaps the deadliest combat outfit in military history." These words were from an article by John G. Hubbell, revealing a new, secret unit called the U.S. NAVY SEALS. It announced the evolution of a needed jungle warfare group of Navy men taken from the famed Underwater Demolition Teams (UDT). Vietnam had created the need, and the Navy's UDT had provided the solution.

The words struck home like the barbs of my black iron trident, now rusting in the garage with the smell of fish on it. As the son of a Navy test pilot, the grandson of a newly retired three-star vice admiral, I had wanted nothing at all to do with the military. But then I read this article about a new secret organization of special warfare professionals in Vietnam that had been unknown until this day. The story of men that scuba dived, jumped from planes, and killed with quiet precision, hit me straight in the heart. The world's largest Navy had only been able to create 200 SEALs so far.

For the first time in my life, a goal began to form. I was going to be a Navy SEAL. It was time to think of my future after high school. Up until now I was just floating along the paths that the Navy sent us. We had changed locations and schools every three years. I had made some friends along the way but had always left them behind. School was easy, but I never fit in. I was always the new guy. I had been encouraged to learn an instrument, so I picked trumpet so I could be the bugler in Boy Scouts. That led to playing in the school bands. I was never very good, but it got me out of the house.

I had always planned to go to college. Everyone in my family did that, so it did not seem very important to plan a career. I had only a few interests that kept me motivated to wake up. They were girls, fishing, sailing, snorkeling, and motorcycles. None of these interests made for much of a future career. My family consisted of great military achievers who had met and worked with great men and world leaders. I knew much would be expected of me, but until reading this story of men working as SEALs and getting paid to do things that I only dreamed of (diving, parachuting, and demolitions), I had spent almost no time wondering what I would do as an adult.

"Dad, how do I get into the Naval Academy?" I had asked honestly. I had found a life goal.

The look on my parents' faces wavered between shock and amazement. Dad sat on the front porch, sipping his always present bourbon and sugar highball, cooking a chicken in the hibachi grill brought home from our last tour of duty in Yokosuka, Japan. As a Naval Academy graduate, career naval aviator, and a World War II Purple Heart recipient, the Navy was his only life. Promotion past captain was not possible, and alcohol was an addiction. His voice, when he spoke, almost trembling.

"Why do you ask?" he said and lit another Lucky Strike.

"I am thinking of going there," I said. "I want to be a SEAL, and if I am going to be in the military, I may as well do it as an officer. The Academy seems like the best way to do that."

Neither my mother nor father had heard anything after "going there." It had been their hope for me for years. I could be the family's fourth generation academy graduate. Neither had ever heard of the SEALs. That did not matter to them. The Naval Academy and West Point had been in our families for four generations of career military men. These soldiers and sailors were all career combat veterans. They also married women of fathers with distinguished careers of service in the Army and the Navy, going back to before the Civil War.

Earlier conversations on the subject had always been met with my adamant insistence that I would never consider the military in any manner or fashion. There was simply nothing about what I knew of the military that was appealing. I had never wanted to fly airplanes onto carriers at sea or drive ships around the world on bounding seas. Most of all I didn't want take orders from anyone about anything.

But now, it was different. I was thinking about a future with an organization that I had never heard of. I had spent very little time thinking about what I wanted to do with my life so far. I had figured that I would have plenty of time in college to figure out a future.

The SEALs had been one big American secret for five years after President Kennedy authorized the Navy to create them from within the current legendary Underwater Demolition Teams in 1962. I had the grades for a scholarship to go to most good colleges, but the Naval Academy would give me a leg up on the civilian college trained ROTC officers I would compete with for promotion in the military.

Equally important, I wanted to go away. I wanted to leave a home where I was sometimes the only barrier between my six-foot alcoholic father and my five-foot mother who was way too often the target of his evening drunken rages. Mom was tough enough to survive without me, and she loved him, despite his many faults, so I did not feel guilty planning to get out as soon as possible.

Five years later, I was a new ensign and a graduate of the U.S. Naval Academy like my father and grandfather before me.

At the Academy, I had learned that my aspirations to special operations were not welcome. This institution had a tradition that mostly trained seamen to fight in ships at sea. It also allowed for some to go to pilot training that would operate off aircraft carriers, and a small percentage that could join the Marines (a branch of the Navy Department) so they could ride the Navy amphibious ships and assault enemy beaches like Guadalcanal.

The SEAL option had only just recently been included. There were no SEALs immortalized among the heroic names engraved in Memorial Hall. No naval history classes spoke of this tiny group of secret warriors. What I learned, I learned on my own. There was no chance to make admiral in this small organization, but I was only looking for a job I could enjoy. One year at a time was all I had wanted to imagine.

Fate would play a role in my choice. The five SEAL slots that were made available to our graduating class of 889 were long gone before I could make a choice for assignment during Service Selection Night. Selection was by class rank, and I was right in the middle. I thought about the marines, but ruled that out after a summer field training event found me picking ticks off every part of my body. So I took what was left. I was going to a destroyer, but first I opted to use my thirty-day "free" graduation leave time to attend Navy dive school.

I arrived in Key West, Florida, with nine other USNA classmates and checked into the bachelor officer quarters (BOQ) there. It was tropical and smelled of flowers. There was blue sky and crystal-clear ocean everywhere I looked. This was a good place to be. I had made it to the first real job of my life and was drawing an ensign's pay with food and housing allowances. I drove my very own used car, which I had purchased in my senior year with money I had made in various little businesses, run under the radar, at old USNA. I felt good. I was twenty-one and on my own.

"Drop maggot!" screamed Instructor Jones.

I fell to the hot, dark cement lot with twin eighty-cubic-foot steel tanks strapped to my newly suntanned back. The rough grey-black straps bit harshly into my collarbones as I struggled up from one push-up after another. The sweat rolled into my eyes in the Key West summer sun, and I was having a ball.

The previous night I had swum in the crystal-clear waters of the Gulf of Mexico, attached by a rope to my swim buddy, while looking around for the Portuguese Man-O-War jellyfish that made all night dives an adventure. I had reveled in the experience. I was swimming in warm ocean waters surrounded by crystalline colors of coral and sea green with fish flowing in and out of view. I was trying to find the telltale antennae of the delicious lobster that hid under the rocks we passed over. It was my intent to come back and get some for dinner that weekend.

That afternoon we were required to do some free diving with just mask and fins. The goal was to free dive down to thirty-five feet and tie a rope around a long pole placed on the bottom near the long dock we were standing on. It was a simple enough task, but it required holding your breath, equalizing ear pressures, and conserving energy as you descended. An instructor was on the bottom with scuba tanks watching for panic from air hunger or the relative darkness that came with depth. He followed us up in case we passed out on the way back to the surface. My time came, and I had no concerns. I had practiced holding my breath in the bathtub for fun, and had achieved my goal of two minutes underwater.

As I floated on top, gazing down at my target, I hyperventilated with deep slow breaths to decrease my carbon dioxide level. It is not the lack of oxygen that makes you crave a breath, it is the increasing carbon dioxide that freaks out the brain and sends the screaming messages to *breathe*. We knew already that, at thirty-three feet down, the water pressure would be double the pressure on the surface. This meant that the air in our lungs and other body parts would be squeezed to fifty percent of its normal volume.

That was Boyles Law, and we had studied that physics formula. One of the problems this creates is in the ear and sinus cavities. They are full of air. The greatest pressure change difference is in the first ten feet. It is critical to hold your nose and blow out while descending to force air through the Eustachian tube into the middle ear space (which is behind your eardrum) and into the eight sinus spaces. If you forget this, then the outside pressure starts to squeeze the air in your head and suck your eardrum backwards in the ear canal. It also starts sucking the mucous membranes of your sinus cavities inward and, as I would soon discover, that can hurt like hell.

I started swimming down, calmly popping air into the appropriate sinus and ear spaces needed to descend without discomfort. I knew to stay ahead of the need. The Eustachian tube has an internal diameter about equal to a human hair, and air will not pass easily if it is inflamed. I made it to the bottom, found the pole, and tied my required knot. I waved to the dive instructor sitting on the bottom, breathing his SCUBA and watching us carefully, and I calmly started my ascent. I knew to blow out a bit of air on the way up, since that lowered the carbon dioxide levels that the brain was sensing. This lessened the need-to-breathe reflex. This was just plain fun.

About halfway to the surface, an unexpected sharp pain started stabbing me above my eyebrows. I could see the surface about fifteen feet up, but the pain was getting worse, so I swallowed. This usually let the expanding air back out of the ear and sinuses. The ears equalized, but the forehead pain got worse, and I mean a *lot* worse! This was new, and the fun was gone. I wanted to stop ascending, but I needed air, so upwards I continued wondering what in the world was causing this. Perhaps I had hit a jellyfish, or maybe a Portuguese man-of-war on the way up? Then, with the bright surface only a few feet away, I heard a squeak, and a *pop* sound in my forehead, and the pain was gone. *Wow, was that nice.*

I hollered out the required "all OK, Instructor" as I surfaced. Something was still not right, however; because my mask was half filled with a warm fluid, and I had to tilt my head up to see the instructor. When I did this, I tasted blood, and I noticed that the fluid in my mask was red. I popped the mask off to find it filled with my own blood still leaking from my nose. The instructor was smiling as he signaled me over to the dock.

"Looks like you have had a sinus squeeze, sir. Nothing to worry about. The bleeding will stop soon. Do you have any pain?"

"No pain, Instructor," I said, amazed. "I had pain ascending, but then it went away after I heard a *pop* in my forehead."

I was washing the large bloody goo collection from my mask.

"Well that *is* good news, but you might want to climb out now since these waters are full of sharks." The diving supervisor sounded amused.

I was out on the deck in seconds! He was correct about sharks, of course, but he was just messing with me. It worked.

"Adams, get over here," leered another instructor nearby. He was dressed in solid olive drab shorts and a similarly starched short sleeve shirt with his name embroidered over one pocket and U.S. NAVY over the other. Above the left pocket sat a huge black embroidered eagle holding a musket, anchor, and a trident. It was a very distinctive large insignia, in all black thread, which meant he was a Navy SEAL. His jungle boots were green canvas with glistening, hand polished black toes.

"Have you ever thought of becoming a Navy SEAL?"

"Yes, Instructor, but they told me at the Academy to forget it. There was no career in special warfare they kept telling me. Besides, all five slots for training were gone before I had a chance to choose that option on service selection night."

"Your advisors were right, sir. You can't make admiral, but *think* about it. We are really trying to hurt you here, and you are having way too much fun. You smile more than the others. That is a very good sign in my humble opinion. Now drop."

I smiled inwardly as thoughts about my high school and academy ambition floated back to me. Someone with credibility thought I might be able to be a SEAL. More importantly, he was looking at me as an officer. The seriousness of that realization had a profound effect on me.

I would just need to figure out how to get there. As I thought about the day, I realized that the encouragement I had received meant more than just recruitment. A first class petty officer with a SEAL tab had seen something he liked. He did not need to say it, but I realized, with a bit of awe, that he was evaluating me as someone he might be asked to follow into combat one day. Damn, that was intimidating to a young, wet-behind-the-ears ensign.

The aging, World War II destroyer, USS *Hamner* (DD-718) was moored to the pier on Treasure Island, San Francisco, at the site of the 1936 World's Fair. The salt air smelled of oil and tar as I climbed the gangplank to report in for duty. I wore a shiny new silver third class divers badge on my khaki uniform as a new graduate of the diving school. Life was about to become very different, but not in an enjoyable way.

My shipboard assignment would begin as the administrative officer working with the personnel specialists, and later as first lieutenant, or deck division officer. The men assigned to the deck division were not the kind of men that I would, one day, hope to marry my daughter. They were paint chippers and brass polishers, and they were mostly undereducated. These men lived in tight quarters below deck that were difficult to like. The air vents that brought them humid and rust-tinged air held plastic packets of marijuana, placed there to allow easy access without accountability. Almost everyone on this ship used illegal drugs, even some of the officers. Vietnam had changed the military for the next two decades to come. We were allowed sideburns and beards, and we were discouraged from wearing uniforms in public to avoid getting spit on by a public made angry by years of a seemingly unjustifiable war.

Destroyer life was difficult. When at sea, a sailor's work day is twenty-four hours long. When tied up at the pier, there is nothing to do except formations, chip paint, and push paperwork. I lived alone in the ship's forward officer's quarters. If our ship ever had a collision at sea, my room would fill with water first. I kept my Navy issue wetsuit under the bunk, and I practiced putting it on in the dark. The loud shrill of the collision alarm drill was the most fearful sound I had ever heard, causing lightning bursts of apprehension, but I could get into that wet suit, in absolute darkness, in a matter of seconds.

I was designated the ship's diver, since I was dive qualified. This allowed me the unusual opportunity to jump over the side of the ship at sea, in the middle of the Pacific Ocean, and help recover training torpedoes which we fired in practice. This was dangerous, and it earned me some "cool points" with the enlisted men. It also allowed me to help conduct an underwater hull survey of the ship when tied to the pier. This required shutting down the engines and going completely to shore power, since the engines had seawater-intake grates that could suck me tight to the hull while I ran out of air and drowned. I did the survey and cleaned the seawater intake grates and loved every minute of it

Blessedly, after twelve months on that destroyer, a message came in. I was doing the jobs I was assigned and was certain that there was no future for me driving ships. I had a five-year service obligation, and I would find a way to serve honorably. I was not spending time thinking about the future. I was simply serving as required, trying to earn the surface warfare insignia by completing the required tasks. There were four more years to go on my service obligation. I would think about the future later.

The message was an ALNAV (addressed to everyone in the Navy and Marine Corps) announcing that the Navy needed SEALs. Tryouts were to be held the next day on our home base – Treasure Island, San Francisco. We were in port, and this was my chance. This was totally unexpected, and I had to slow my spinning thoughts down just to absorb what I was reading, and what it might mean for me. I knew what I needed to do.

I went up to senior officer's quarters, found my department head, and informed him that I would like to take this test. It was during the workday tomorrow, but after an enthusiastic explanation of the ALNAV and my intent, he granted me permission to go.

I was not really asking permission, I thought with a disrespectful inward smile, as I walked away. Nothing, short of God interfering personally, was going to keep me from this chance.

At the recruiting meeting, they showed the recently produced 1969 U.S. Navy recruiting movie entitled *Men with Green Faces*. This was the first time that I saw, up close and personal, what a SEAL did for a living. I could hardly contain my excitement. It showed men shivering, and enduring, covered with mud, in very difficult training, which then led to a job where they paid them extra to jump, dive, swim, shoot, and sneak through the jungles.

The men in the film looked older, focused, and fierce. They were swimming out of submarines in crystal waters at night. They were moving silently through jungle overgrowth with black and green painted faces, using hand signals to communicate, and they carried weapons that looked lethal, with bands of ammunition draped over their shoulders like Mexican banditos.

There was music and quieted outboard motor noises blended into scenes of rubber boats, loaded with low-lying armed men, sliding along dark, dirty, overgrown rivers. I could barely control my breathing. It was even more exciting than the *Readers Digest* article had suggested to my sixteen-year-old self. The movie made it clear that there would be a great challenge and some suffering involved, but I knew then, almost as well as I know today, that the human being has a grand ability to suffer and endure.

The physical fitness test that followed was not difficult for me. We swam 300 yards, using an underwater recovery stroke (like breast stroke or side stroke), did sit-ups, push-ups, squat thrusts, and then ran one and a half miles in boots. I was an average athlete at the Academy, but I passed easily. I had always been an avid swimmer, and lacrosse had been my sport since high school, so running was not unpleasant. I had tried wrestling and liked it because it complemented the judo training I did in my younger days. Interestingly, I would discover later that lacrosse and wrestling were statistically the sports that best prepared men for training.

LT Scotty Lyons oversaw the testing. Helping him, and in charge of the testing, was a BUD/S instructor by the name of Steve Frisk. I would meet them both again. They both wore their working uniforms, but they had rows of ribbons above their top breast pockets that screamed that they had seen combat up close and personal. LT Lyons was an older man for his rank. His hair was grayish, but his arms were tanned and rippled. I winced at the strength in his hand when I shook it.

I would learn later that, during one of his squad's Vietnam patrols, they had captured documents from the enemy dead. They were training documents, and the translators sent them back after translation, highlighting a special sentence referring to the SEALs. It read, "…but above all, beware of those men with green faces, who come from nowhere, and go nowhere." Thus, the movie title *Men with Green Faces*. And here was LT Lyons himself, showing it to all that would watch.

LT Lyons had led one of the most successful SEAL combat units ever, they were known as the Barefoot Patrol. Since SEALs operated behind enemy lines, boot prints would give them away. So Scotty and his patrol operated in native flip flops, without shoes. He would later be our class's first phase officer, but he would not remember me or most of the hundreds he had screened. Petty Officer Frisk's Vietnam operational photos hung in the training area. He would be one of our instructors.

"I will see you soon at training, sir," I said as I walked up to LT Lyons with hope and confidence.

"That's nice, Ensign," he said, totally unimpressed.

He knew what I did not. Most trainees fail. Only one in five students will graduate from any new training class, then and now.

It was 1600 (4 PM) when I made it back to the admin office aboard ship. I waltzed into the office where I worked and found three of my men there, planning their departure for the day.

"Stop whatever you are doing," I said. "One of you pull the regulations for application to SEAL training. One of you start filling it out from my personnel records, and the last one of you draft the letter for our commander's approval for transfer. Oh, by the way, we are not going home today until all of this is done. So, let's go."

They knew where I had gone that day, and they jumped to the tasks. Either they were happy for me, or they were happy to get rid of me. I like to think it was the former, since they had taught me how to function in a dysfunctional environment, and we all got along well, mostly because I listened to them. The post-Vietnam military was *not* a normal organization. It was broken in so many ways that no one tried very hard to fix it anymore. We were allowed to grow beards and mustaches like the old wooden ship days. None of us realized that the application process would take six more months, as my commanding officer would require a replacement before letting me go. I was the ship's junior officer, and I held the unenviable title of SLJO which stood for "Shitty Little Jobs Officer." Replacing me would not be hard, it would just take time.

I used the time to start working out again. I found a pipe in the communications center that was perfect for pull-ups, so I stopped there every day to the amusement of the crew. I did my push-ups wherever I could and noticed that it was harder on a ship at sea. As the ship came up when I was pushing up, gravity added to the effort. Swimming and running were reserved for in-port time, and luckily our sea voyages were usually to Honolulu, which only took five days. Then there were warm tropical days and nights waiting to let me sweat whenever I wanted.

It would take six more agonizing months of sea duty before I received orders to Basic Underwater Demolition/SEAL training in Coronado, California. Like hot molten lead dripping slowly down my skin, they were the longest six months of my life so far, but they would serve me well. More than once in the gut-wrenching pain and biting polar cold of training, I would be faced with the possibility that I would fail. It was at those times that I would lift my filthy, shivering, mud-covered head and peek over the sand dunes to see the distant gray ships at sea; they seemed like shadows of my past soul-consuming demons. There was no doubt in my mind then that I would die trying before I would go back to that ship. I could summon almost Herculean strength at times like that. It was blessed motivation, and for that I will always be grateful for my time at sea.

And for all the training I had done during those six interminable months, I did not train even close to hard enough.

"Pain is temporary. Quitting lasts forever."
—Lance Armstrong

Chapter 3
Pre-training

Pre-training is an unofficial period that begins when a trainee reports to the BUD/S training facility and ends once Phase One begins. Trainees are in a holding status, and no one can fail. This time is used to learn how to run and swim and perform physical training (PT). Some trainees were rollbacks from earlier classes, like PN2 Mike Suter, our soon-to-be class senior enlisted man, and others would be there for a few weeks, or a few days, depending on how their transfer orders were written. More time was always better.

Typically, pre-training lasts four weeks and consists entirely of physical training, swimming instruction with and without fins, obstacle course familiarization, physical exercises, and lots of running.

It would start in two days at the leisurely hour of 0600, and the instructors would not be fearsome at all. They were downright encouraging and friendly. That would change after the orientation phase, and they would remind us of that quite regularly. Our class proctor was an instructor, there for the duration of our training, to act as a liaison and advocate. He was a Vietnam veteran with stories that were hard to believe. We only heard them when he was drunk, which was often on weekends. If only half of what he said he did was true, then there were things done over there that would likely never be written about.

Pre-training was a time to meet each other, discuss what we did not know, and plan for the day we would shave our heads and take the first steps towards hoped for graduation. We wore white tee shirts and standard-issue green starched hats to distinguish us from the true trainees in green shirts with green, red, or blue helmet liners. The color of the helmet liners changed from green, to red, to blue as they progressed through the three phases of training. Red and blue helmet liners were what we sought. They would mean that we had finished Hell Week, the great equalizer. We would begin to find our physical strengths and weaknesses, and work on them individually. There were at least seventy men ready to go, but most would not make it. Only eleven survivors would stand in dress blue uniforms at graduation.

The training that would begin after this four-week pre-training phase would last six months and would be divided into three phases.

First Phase (eight weeks): Physical training, that includes Hell Week, with time planned to recover before starting Second Phase.

Second Phase (eight weeks): Land Warfare training in weapons and demolition.

Third Phase (nine weeks): Diving training in SCUBA, mixed gas and pure oxygen diving, and underwater mission operations.

Currently, training has swapped Phases Two and Three to allow land warfare to be the final Third Phase. Some expected losses in the dive phase now happen earlier in training. These twenty-five weeks constitute basic BUD/S, but to earn and wear the SEAL insignia, each man remains at the training center for one more year of advanced SEAL training. Then they receive orders to their first SEAL Team.

Each enlisted trainee from our class was given a shared room in the attached barracks with the Pacific Ocean sounds pounding in through the open windows. Officers stayed at the BOQ or in rented housing if married. Behind the barracks, there was a narrow sand beach with a rock jetty jutting from behind the legendary Hotel Del Coronado, just one mile further north. It scarred the scenery as it pushed out into the Pacific Ocean. Our training class would become intimate with those rocks on a dark night during our first night of Hell Week. Injuries would play a role in our graduation numbers.

Surrounded by sand and asphalt, these standard barracks rooms all had stories to tell. The whispers of tormented men and the echoes of automatic weapons were faintly discernable to the imagination. The polished linoleum floors were pock-marked from 7.62 mm hot shell casings fired from weapons used to signal the gut wrenching start of Hell Weeks past. Most of the men there had never seen a weapon that could fire such a devastating explosive barrage at the unthinkable rate of over 600 rounds per minute.

We were all young and enthusiastic. Some had no real clue why they were there or what they had signed up for. It was still classified stuff we were going to train for. One recruit found out he was sent there by mistake. I did not know much at all about what was ahead and neither did most anyone else.

As noted earlier, Personnelman Second Class (PN2) Mike Suter had joined our group in pre-training as a rollback from his prior class. Those already assigned to this early group – those who had the sense to pay attention – learned some of what to expect from training. This would be his third BUD/S class assignment. It was a winter class, and he was not happy about that. He had planned carefully to avoid that fate again, but the recent class rollback changed him from summer to winter training. Damn.

To PN2 Suter, a Navy ship always smelled like a mix of old paint, stale cigarette smoke, and rancid oil and sweat. It permeated clothing, skin, and hair. It could be washed away, but it was impossible to forget. The work required to maintain the grey welded matrix of steel floating in corrosive salt seas is never-ending. The hundreds of men who eat, sleep, and labor all day and night to keep it combat ready meld into a constant ant hill of activity like the incessantly active and noisy fuel-oil-fed boilers in its bowels. The days and nights at sea only differ if you make it to the bridge or outer parts of the ship and note the sun or stars reflected off the water that it floats (and rolls nauseatingly) in.

Responsibility is sometimes daunting, for life-and-death risk taking is part of activities aboard ship. Underway refueling, with lines stretching between ships underway, navigation through rocky shoals, travel over storm-driven waves as high as the ship's mast, and fear of the unknown when an alarm sounds signaling "man overboard" or "collision" make danger part of every day. Sailors drift from eight-hour watch to eight-hour watch until night falls. The first watch of the new day is broken into two four-hour watches. The mid-watch begins at midnight and ends at 0400. The next watch is 0400 to 0800 (and this one is the hardest since fatigue is real), and the next workday still starts at 0800.

The day PN2 Mike Suter left the ship for BUD/S again, the weight of the world seemingly lifted off his shoulders. To leave the clinging, oily smell and excessive demands of others behind and undertake a personal challenge that he knew he could not fail (a challenge imagined but not yet fully understood) was a cleansing experience. It was irrelevant that he did not know some of what was ahead. He did know precisely what he was escaping. He was going to try a second time now. The East Coast winter ice and snow had destroyed his dreams last time

There was a bubbly excitement inside him as he prepared for the months ahead. Life was so much simpler now. He was responsible only for himself, and that was a feeling like walking on air. No more watches to stand or men to supervise. He knew himself well. He believed in himself. He had already endured life challenges that few could comprehend, and he had made it through one Hell Week day of the coldest on record. He would get another chance soon, and he felt good about that. He lit another Marlboro red and dragged deeply.

He was self-sufficient and embarking on a journey that had first been planned four years ago. He was certain that the future would add a great big, gaudy, golden Budweiser-like Navy SEAL insignia. Of that he had little doubt. He was being given another chance, and he would earn it. This was critical to the psychological needs of a man once again on his own and solely responsible for the success or failure waiting ahead. Suffering, luckily, was not a stranger to him, and that would serve him well. Only injury or death could prevent his success this time.

On the first weekly four-mile timed training run during pre-training, each runner needed to finish in thirty-two minutes, wearing long pants tucked into green canvas jungle boots, running along the wet, sandy beach edge. Not all the class had reported in yet, but so far ENS Johnson and FTG3 Frank Winget were the best runners. Frank had run the one- and two-mile races on his high school track team. Running was not a problem for either of them. They both looked like runners, with thin defined leg muscles and gaunt but muscular upper bodies. They finished almost side by side in twenty-seven minutes, well ahead of the pack. This was Frank's second and last try. No one knew that he had quit Class 72 eighteen months ago. He was calm and quietly confident, watching his new classmates finish one at a time.

ENS John Johnson was lean and fit and outweighed the leaner Frank by twenty pounds. His blond hair was cut short, and his side burns were shorter than the regulations required. He was smiling and did not look very tired when the rest of us straggled across the finish line in various stages of exhaustion. He was thinking about graduating already, but it was not to be.

When he decided to quit after completing Hell Week, it surprised everyone. He had to create an event that would not make it his fault. So, at the top of the thirty-foot rope-ladder obstacle, after another fast time on the course, he climbed over the top log, felt his feet hook safely in the heavy rope squares, paused, and he let go with his hands. He fell hard onto the sand below with a loud and nauseating *thump* while classmates watched in horror. He knew he might be injured. He even knew he might die, but that would be better than the ignominy of telling his classmates he did not feel he could go on another five months. There were problems with his girl, and this was just one stressor too much for the challenges ahead.

Frank Winget had again lead the run that day. He was back from the fleet, having quit his previous Hell Week in its second day. He was mortified by his decision and shared this fact with no one. His life until the Navy had been one of relative poverty with a single mother and siblings. He still helped support them when he could with money sent home. He was an exceptional runner and could swim well. Past training had not been difficult until the icy exhaustion of Hell Week had snuck up and slapped him upside the head. He had been swayed by the officer that had quit with him at the same time. Even now, looking back, he could not fully understand why he gave up and rang the bell three times. He had not been ready for the full-on assault he had been faced with, but he was ready now. The bell would never be in his future again. Of that he was sure.

"Twenty-seven minutes flat, Winget. Splendid job," called the timekeeper as he loped past the finish line.

Winget smiled, knowing that he could have done better. As he walked off the run and let the sweat dry, he reflected on how lucky he had been to get another chance.

To get another shot at training, he had been required to submit a NAVPERS Personnel Action Request asking for the transfer. At every level of his shipboard chain of command his request was denied. With this piece of career-ending paper in his hand, he had made his way across the bay back to the training compound in Coronado. There he met with CDR Tom Tarbox, the commanding officer. He presented himself formally to the commander and stated his case for returning. He showed the disapproved request paper, restated his desire to return, and with all the professionalism he could muster, convinced CDR Tarbox of his sincerity.

"Give me that form, sailor" CDR Tarbox almost growled. He then boldly wrote his own recommendation at the bottom. "Strongly recommended for acceptance to BUD/S training!" and signed the form.

"Now go back to your ship and submit that. It might just work now. I hope it does because I think you are ready this time, and we can still use you. Good luck."

Almost as fast as the mail could make things happen, FTC3 Winget had orders off his ship and across the wonderful, welcoming waters of Glorietta Bay to BUD/S Class 81. He smiled at the memory.

Bringing up the rear, just past the thirty-two-minute mark was the slightly paunchy, beans-and-tortilla-fed (but determined) Petty Officer Third Class Frank "Rosy" Rosensweig. He was handsome, had a ruddy complexion, and was slightly overweight, like many in his Hispanic family. He did not like to run or swim very much, but he had learned to do both well because he planned to join the Navy, earn a living, and see the world. No one had ever thought he would even graduate high school. But he did. And now he would show them what *else* he could do.

His motivation was known only to himself. He wanted to prove something. He had grown up in relative poverty, and his family had very little to offer him. Education was important, but the cost of college was too great to consider. He would find another way. The Navy offered him income, independence, and opportunity. The SEALs were an afterthought for Rosy who had never run four miles in his life when he volunteered.

One by one, the class straggled in, and a list was made. The best and worst runners were identified, and the instructors gathered to impress all that the standard must be met.

"Failures over here for a Monster Mash."

And with that, the class split into two sections.

"Take a seat and watch your classmates run the sand dunes while I remind you that the thirty-two-minute time you just made will be cut back to thirty minutes by the end of training, and it appears there are some sand dunes in many of your futures if you do not keep improving."

Monster Mash was a term used to describe punishment for any perceived failure. Sometimes it was required of the entire class. Sometimes it was used to encourage quitting, by threatening to continue until someone quit.   It always *sucked*.

"Strive not to be a success, but rather to be of value."
—Albert Einstein

Chapter 4

Reporting in for Pre-training, BUD/S Training Center, Coronado, California

The quarterdeck was manned by an enlisted sentry in his blue dress uniform. He sat behind a standard issue grey metal desk with a darker grey rubber-ized top. A small plaque sat in front of him labeled "Quarterdeck." Every ship in the navy has a quarterdeck area which guards access to a ship via a gangplank walkway. There is always a sailor of the watch guarding this one access point, as a place to render honors to visitors or confirm access rights.

Many naval buildings, with a commanding officer in residence, have a quarterdeck entrance area. This is the case at BUD/S. The American flag hung majestically limp just inside the double glass entry doors next to a dark blue and gold Navy flag. If you looked behind the desk he manned, another glass door stood propped open, and there were a few green helmets lined neatly side by side on the covered sidewalk that merged with a large unenclosed area of black asphalt.

The training center is now named proudly for CAPT Phil H. Bucklew, the official "Father of Naval Special Warfare." He served in the first special warfare units in World War II, where he twice earned the Navy Cross medal, the second highest combat award in the Navy. To get there you need to drive over the Coronado Bay Bridge from San Diego, or drive the entire length of the Silver Strand from Imperial Beach, eight miles south, which is only minutes from the border crossing into Tijuana, Mexico. The mud flats training area, where trainees spend some gloriously unpleasant, foul, and smelly days, is just along the California border with Mexico, part of the Tijuana River estuary.

The sentry today was watching the quarterdeck area with bored indifference. ENS John Muggs paused at the glass doors because, standing next to the entrance, was a life-sized plastic Creature from the Black Lagoon with glaring yellow eyes, mouth open threateningly, with two upper fangs glinting in the sunlight. Its right arm held a long white pole with a trident shaped sign attached to the tip that read "So, you wanna be a frogman?" It wore a faded green web belt, and hanging from its left side, was a K-bar knife sheath without knife. Its feet were huge and webbed. Its hands were webbed and had long claws on each of five fingerlike projections.

John figured it was designed to be somewhat intimidating, but it didn't scare him one bit. Instead, it made him happy.

It appeared to be a faded green scale-covered artifact from the 1954 3D black and white monster movie *Creature from the Black Lagoon* about a strange prehistoric beast that lurked in the depths of the Amazonian jungle. Examining it made him smile. He was where he wanted to be, and it was far from the many Golden Glove boxing rings of his past. Later, he heard that some past frogmen had appropriated it for this somewhat intimidating display.

Behind him roared the traffic from the Silver Strand Boulevard as it whizzed past the entrance to Coronado and the Naval Amphibious Base across the way. Visible in the sandy lot far to the left was an equally impressive obstacle course. There was a thirty-foot set of telephone poles sticking up with a heavy, slightly frayed, well-used, rope cargo net strung between the poles. It looked just like the cargo nets seen in World War II movies when marines went over the sides of ships en route to an amphibious beach assault by boats. Up close, it smelled like tar and sweat. It made him smile with anticipation. He was an athlete, and he felt happy. Soon he would be spending time in the sun and surf, climbing that rope obstacle, and responsible only to himself.

He glanced at his reflection in the standard-issue military metal and glass doors and liked what he saw. There was nothing amiss, and all the brass uniform accoutrements shined appropriately. He removed his khaki garrison cap with his right hand, tucked it smartly under his web belt, glanced at his reflected image in the glass one last time, and pulled open the right-side door. He wandered in looking as officer-like as he could. He presented himself with authority to the sentry and showed his orders.

"Ensign Muggs reporting for training," he sounded off firmly.

He stood five-foot ten inches tall at 182 pounds, his khaki uniform was pressed, an ensign's shiny gold bars were centered perfectly on the shirt collars, and the nametag above the opposite pocket was buffed and waxed with Pledge polish. His "gig line" was straight, but he saw the sentry check it anyway as he stood up. The *gig line* is the imaginary line made by the shirt edge, belt buckle, and pants zipper flap. The waist where the shirt met the belt was free of wrinkles and the excess shirt cloth was folded backwards on each side, at the waist, to give a more chiseled effect. The Naval Academy had taught him well. He looked good for a "butter-bar" ensign, and his chiseled boxing features impressed the sentry who stood and saluted.

He had closed the metal top right drawer quickly as he stood up to salute. There was a soda can nestled in the front corner with brown spit stuck to the can's edge. He had a few tiny specks of black stuck to his upper teeth, despite his quick move to drop it in the can while John had been outside admiring himself. His thumb and finger were rubbing together quickly to remove any telltale residue of Copenhagen snuff. It kept him awake, and he used it even though it was said it also contained finely ground fiberglass to cause microscopic lip cuts and aid the nicotine absorption.

"Yes sir," the sentry said, after having his salute returned, and consulting a list on his standard issue steel desk, while rising from his equally standard-issue grey metal chair. He was dressed in a dress blue wool winter uniform and covered with a white Dixie Cup hat. His shoulder sleeve bore the three white diagonal stripes of a seaman. His salute had been casual, but correct.

"You are assigned to BUD/S Class 81, sir. And you will need to see the admin officer. He is down the hall there on your right."

There would be over seventy sailors in this next class, and he was not paying any attention as one after another wandered in on their own schedules. His time as a trainee was coming also, but he was not yet assigned to a class. He was just bored and waiting for the shift to end.

Much of the front desk watch staff was made up of men rolled back from a previous class of trainees as they waited for an injury to heal. John heard the top drawer open again, and the seat cushion hiss, as he moved away down the hall.

A large, intimidating, neatly tanned man passed by him. He nodded as he passed.

"Sir."

As he passed the quarterdeck, he heard the chair scrape quickly back and heard the seaman again.

"Hooyah, Instructor Thornton."

There was no response. This instructor had not yet reported in for duty as our class instructor, but everyone knew who he was. His name was unfamiliar to John then, but books would be written about him and his awe-inspiring exploits in Vietnam that won him the Medal of Honor.

It was a typical narrow military hallway with a buffed linoleum floor and lined along the sides with open gray metal doors that led to small offices. But there was a sense of specialness reflected in the pictures on the walls. The pictures depicted tanned men in khaki bathing suits with nothing but a K-bar knife on their faded green web belts; sky scenes with parachutists floating on air; and darker underwater photos of scuba divers following the dull fluorescent nuclear glow of a compass board. A green canvas duffel bag sat on the floor where someone coming (or going) had left it. It was stenciled with a name and rank, but he did not pause to read it. He felt a bit like tiptoeing, unsure if he really belonged.

At the same time, Ensigns Stan Holloway and Mike Turk were across the street trying to get rooms at the bachelor officers' quarters (BOQ). Both were big, powerful men, and the desk clerk was appropriately impressed. Neither had met before. Both wore polyester civilian clothes, purchased at Navy Exchanges, which stocked simple inexpensive clothing for men with little civilian style awareness. Stan's clothes were marked XXL and Mike's was marked XL. They both noticed the difference, but it was Mike that was wondering about the older, larger ensign and whether he could swim very fast or far.

"I am reporting to BUD/S training," Stan said to the clerk with an authority learned from his years of Army experience.

He was wearing the uniform of a new Navy ensign, but his previous uniform had been an Army one, with the black embroidered double bars of a captain, and a ranger tab on his sleeve above his unit insignia. He had worn those proudly on his Army battle dress uniform (BDU). He had transferred services and started over again in rank for this chance to do something very different.

The first SEAL he had met in jump school with him had seemed absolutely bulletproof. He was impressed and envious, so now he was seeking that same confidence and capability. He checked out the man to his right and saw a slightly younger, fit, quiet professional who carried himself with a confident surety. He knew that he could swim just fine, but he had yet to discover how far.

"Me too," Mike noted with pleasure, as they sized each other up.

Stan was taller, he observed as he reached his hand out. His grip was firm and muscular, but Mike's was as strong after having already completed the demanding Green Beret Army course. He was quiet and reserved, and meeting Stan was simply a distraction now. His focus was to get moved in, settled, and make his was across the street to check in. Even so, he found himself thinking about who was senior, and since Stan was obviously the older one, it was likely he would be able to hide behind him in training, if he made it. He knew from his own past Army special operations experience that seniority brought expectations and attention. Attention was not something Mike was seeking. His own research had revealed that roughly only twenty percent of the trainees would graduate in an average class. So, one of them was likely not going to make it. He was sure that meant Stan was just someone he would get to know only for a fleeting time because *he* personally was going to graduate.

Stan felt the same way, but after his time in the Army, he had learned that, until he checked in, his time was his own, and he was going to use every bit of this day to get ready. He would report in at the end of the workday so they would have little chance of screwing with him until tomorrow. He still needed to visit the nearby Navy exchange and pick up some uniform insignia and such. He was still learning how to wear a Navy uniform correctly, and he knew there would be someone there to help. He had seen a marine in his khaki uniform earlier and had a moment of panic when he noticed the gold bars were aligned differently than his. A quick retreat and glance at another Navy man in uniform seemed to indicate that the Navy wore their collar insignia differently. Still, it would be a promising idea to verify this. It was reassuring when he noted also that ENS Turk wore his insignia the same way. Neither realized, at the time, that they shared past Army experiences.

They shook hands, passed copies of their orders to the clerk, and got their keys. Mike Turk rushed to his new car, a Datsun 240-Z, to get his bags, and Stan dragged his well-worn bag to the waiting area to pour his free cup of coffee and examine the map of the area hanging on the wall. No hurry today. The adventure would come soon enough. Ranger training was the most difficult event in his life so far, and it was life altering. His confidence in his abilities was absolute, but he knew that the training ahead would be very, very different.

He had smelled and then spied the large coffee urn on the counter across the room, and he noticed the urn's glowing red light and that the brown glass tube was half-filled, indicating that it still held hot coffee. This would be his first stop en route to his room. Coffee powered the Navy (and the Army), and now he wanted some power. He sipped the coffee, his suitcase at his feet, and looked around. There was a very nautical theme to what he saw, and it was appealing but unfamiliar. Life so far had been full of unexpected challenges, and standing in a Navy BOQ, waiting for another chance to prove to the world that he was tougher than most, was clearly a bit surprising as he looked back at where he thought he would be by now. The clock clicked and read 10:06. There was still plenty of time for what he needed to do.

Nearby, in the bachelor enlisted quarters, two black sailors were already checked in for Class 81. These African American class members knew they were up against the odds, as there were very few black frogmen, for reasons no one could explain.

Navy Chief Bernard Waddell wrote about his experiences as one of the first black frogmen in his book, *I Am Somebody*, but this would not be published until 1986. He graduated in 1956 with Class 16E; the E signifying that he did his training on the East Coast at the Naval Amphibious Base Little Creek. That base is still home to all the East Coast SEAL Teams, but training has been only in California since 1971.

Vietnam would officially end while we were in training, and stories of SEALs and their exploits were still only whispered among those with a need to know. Our class proctor was a chief petty officer who was rumored to be one of the "baddest" Vietnam SEALs ever, but his job now was to get us ready to start and survive training. He liked to drink, and he *really* liked to fight. Monday mornings often found him in formation admiring the healing cuts on his hands and knuckles while he smiled at the momentous time he had experienced that weekend. The police knew him by sight and name. They also knew of his wartime record and did not want him in their jail. So mostly, they just made sure he got home safely and did not kill anyone stupid enough to think they could fight him.

My uncle, CAPT Ted Smedberg, was commanding an aviation squadron at North Island Naval Air Station and lived in Coronado. As soon as I arrived, I paid him a visit. It turned out that he was anxious to speak with me. He needed to tell me why I should immediately reconsider SEAL training. He took me out back, and we sat on his picnic table under a fruit tree.

"Bob, in my last job I worked directly for the Chief of Naval Operations (CNO) and was tasked with sending missions directly to the SEALs in Vietnam. Trust me when I tell you this, those guys are just plain crazy."

He went on to share that the chain of command for their missions was shortened for operational reasons and that the CNO could pass a mission directly to a SEAL commander in the field. Ted was the officer tasked to make this happen. My uncle's well-meant cautioning, however, only served to excite me more.

I would learn later that Uncle Ted's father – my grandfather – had actively opposed the idea of forming SEAL teams in the Navy. My grandfather was a three-star vice admiral and Chief of Naval Personnel when the Navy was asked to consider forming SEAL teams. My grandfather adamantly suggested that the Army take on that special operations mission since they already had the Green Berets. He was overruled by his boss, the CNO, ADM Arleigh Burke, who would later have a class of destroyers named after him. Looking back, I remain amazed how hard my family had tried to keep me from my dream.

The day came during pre-training when we decided to make a statement and shave our heads a week before we were required to. Team building. It was

Sunday afternoon, and we met in the barracks as a class to get pumped for the week ahead. I had an electric barber razor that I had used to make money cutting hair in the past. My first used car was bought with the seventy-five-cent haircuts given to many over the years. It was a weekend party feeling as we dared each other to walk away from the shears. Blond, black, and curly hair floated to the floor as we took on the look we would be required to wear in training. Simple shaved heads were easy to care for, but it would kick the crap out of our dating future for the next six months.

Real training was to begin in a week, and we were trying to build a sense of team. No one knew for sure what was coming, but we all knew it was going to be much more difficult than any of us could imagine. Frank Winget and Mike Suter had both made it to Hell Week with previous classes. Frank was keeping this fact to himself out of embarrassment, and there would be no question of quitting this time. Mike was older and in a position of authority as senior enlisted, so he was more open and encouraging. They both had a leg up on the rest of us, and they would be very helpful in the trial ahead.

The gathering of new friends and future water warriors was infused with emotion. Fear, anticipation, excitement, and dread mixed evenly through a room full of men who had chosen to be tested. We had chosen to do what none of us could fully comprehend. We were going to be letting our instructors push us beyond the limits of imagined human endurance. We were all volunteers, and most of us actively wished for a test just like this. Most had played high school or college sports and had been pushed by coaches as best they could. These experiences would be useful, but there would be much more physical and mental exertions required soon. We would discover something about ourselves that few ever learn because the life *most* people choose would never require the revelations ahead. Most of us were raring to go.

Monday would begin our last week as happy "tadpoles" with instructors as our friends and mentors. Soon, First Phase of training would begin, and Hell Week would begin the legendary fourth week of that phase. We could not wait. Some would sit in anticipation of the unknown, knowing in their souls that they would not be able to cross the line into the abyss and emerge again. These predetermined failures were to be expected because, up until now, their lives had been pleasant. They had not yet endured a major life disaster, worked hard for a living wage, or experienced psychological pain. They all had somewhere else to go.

They would fail because there was an escape clause in their brains. They were strong enough and capable enough to do anything that was asked of them, but they had other priorities in their lives. They had a way out that they could live with. Some had money and some had a woman who loved them. Most simply had not been tested by life, and failed, before.

Past challenges or failures provide a psychological protection from future failures, and without this slight advantage, when the limit of perceived human endurance was approached, it would prove too hard to embrace and move past. These trainees would have more comfortable options, and so they would walk away, with purpose, to the ever-present and sometimes haunting brass bell and ring it three times. The bell had a significance of its own to each trainee. Some saw it a symbol of strength that they would be allowed to ring in defiance and celebration on graduation day. Others saw it as a grim and unforgettable reminder of a past failure or the loss of a friend and classmate. To some, it rang in their dreams, causing them to wake in a sweat.

I had learned about Hell, up close and personal. I had become an adult too early. Even today when asked about my teenage years, I comment that I did not have any.

I had a paper route at twelve years old, pulling a wagon stacked high with thick *Washington Post* papers, and I placed the papers on the front steps to each house. The dark, bitter, and often bleak mornings, sometimes with snow, intimidated me as I climbed high steps to get to a porch. Fear of the dark was slowly overcome at an early age. Work built character at a time when character was hard to find. This youthful willingness to work, master fear, and learn independence would prove to be an asset later. I would eventually discover that there was very little an instructor would do that could intimidate me. By the time I made it to BUD/S, I had been harassed and threatened by many more powerful foes.

"More men fail through lack of purpose
than lack of talent."
—Bill Sunday

Chapter 5
First phase begins – 0430 on the "grinder"

0430 came soon enough for most of us. Pre-dawn physical training (PT) hit
with a vengeance, as first phase began. We were in our clean, starched, olive
drab pants with white T-shirts tucked into matching olive drab pants, held up
by black web belts, cinched tightly by shiny, scratch-free, polished buckles.
The brass belt half-inch end piece was positioned exactly at the edge of the
buckle. Our boots reflected moonshine in the dark, as instructors roared
commands with a harshness most were unaccustomed to. Our proctor, Chief
Wade Puckett, was there to watch over his class.

"Mr. Turk, give me the report for your class," ordered an instructor,

"Instructor Frisk, BUD/S Class 81 is formed and ready. All men present
and accounted for," he replied with authority.

"Very well, Mr. Turk, have your class fall in on the grinder for PT,"
ordered Frisk.

He smiled in anticipation as this new class scrambled to comply. His steel
eyes and jet-black hair accented a tall runner's frame. His hair would speckle
grey before his decades of service ended, and he would guide nineteen classes
through First Phase and Hell Week.

We stumbled forward as an organized group of ready and excited men.
We lined up in front of the wooden PT platform in military rows, awaiting

the first PT commands. The instructors circled and waited for weakness to show. The physical weaknesses would be addressed quickly and with enthusiasm. Play time was over. PT was conducted with enthusiasm as we had been trained, but now failure in technique or ability was treated harshly.

Sets of repeating four-count jumping jacks, push-ups, sit-ups, windmills, pull-ups, dips, neck rotations, "hello dollies," flutter kicks, stretches, and more came at us fast. The instructor calling out the exercises from the platform was doing each exercise with us and smiling like he loved it, which he did. This went on for an hour, and a few substandard performers were made to hit the tub. It was real now.

Flutter kicks would become one of our nemeses. We would lay flat with hands under our butts and flutter our straight legs to a four count. The stomach muscles burned with strain as the feet were prohibited from touching ground. We did not like the pain, and we often tried to rest when the instructors looked elsewhere. Unfortunately, there was more than one instructor watching our events. Someone got caught every time. And, after a brief time, the focus was on me and a few others with the start of every flutter kick event. They expected us to give in, and we rarely disappointed them. The penalties were such that it would have been much better if we had spent our spare time doing flutter kicks instead of sleeping.

There was a bathtub full of water next to the PT podium. At any time, when a trainee failed an exercise, an instructor would order us to "hit the tub." We would then jump up and splash deep into the tub, soaking our uniform, socks and boots in the icy water. After a few days in a row of my personal trips to the tub for failing at flutter kicks, an instructor was often heard to say, "Next exercise is flutter kicks, Mr. Adams hit the tub... ready, begin." My failure was thus announced to all in advance. Today was happily *not* one of those days.

Following PT, our class was gathered, in formation, on the same, bleak asphalt "grinder" ready to continue our first day of real training. The weeks of pre-training were over. Our heads were shaved clean, and the instructors were not our friends any more. They *were* yesterday, as they encouraged fitness, wellness, and strength. They had spent eight hours a day teaching us how to do PT properly, run in boots and soft boot-sucking sand, swim efficiently with and without fins, and build up our arms, legs, neck, and stomach muscles to the point where training could begin with less risk of injury. Some of us had been there four or more weeks and some only a week. Not everyone was yet sure they wanted to be there.

"I want the officers over here," rumbled a deep voice from behind.

Eight mostly intimidated and slightly scared officers fell out and ran to the sound of his demand. We were all dressed the same, in starched olive drab fatigue pants that made a harsh, starched scratching noise when we walked, black web belts with shined brass buckles aligned exactly with the pants zipper. Matching white T-shirts were tucked in, and our last name was stenciled on the left breast in black spray paint. We all wore officer helmets with last names stenciled on the front in small white readable capital letters to match the two-inch-wide white stripe down the middle. None of our outfits were wet or dirty, yet.

Two of the officers were less scared than the rest. ENS Mike Turk and ENS Stan Holloway had heard it all before. Just a few months ago, Turk was an Army Green Beret captain. His dress uniform had senior parachutist wings above his pocket which made him different. His old Army uniform was made jauntier by the Special Forces Green Beret, having already completed the legendary Green Beret training. He had been tested, and he knew intimidation. Even so, now he wore the uniform of a Navy ensign and was taking the next test in his own plan to see what else he was made of. He was strong and stood tall amongst the line of men. He knew that he would start and finish training as the class leader since he had been told his date of rank was the earliest.

He did not tell anyone that the sound of waves, crashing in the distance behind him, was intimidating. He could run and jump and shoot well. He could swim well, but he had not spent much time in the almost glacial salt water pounding the beach behind him.

To his right was another large, powerful, blond ex-Army officer who had also worn the rank of captain. They were friends now. ENS Holloway's left uniform arm had sported an Army Ranger tab, and he had worn the Airborne Ranger black beret. He had just been selected for the rank of Army major when his request to transfer was approved, but his date of rank to Army captain was later than Captain Turk's. He would be next in line for class leader. He had already completed jump school at Ft. Benning.

Ranger training was much tougher though, with an average forty percent graduation rate, and it tested endurance and leadership in starvation survival conditions. Wintery weather was a familiar training environment that he had already proven able to endure. His time growing up on a Wyoming cattle ranch had also taught him all about arduous work, and he planned to go back there one day.

The graduation rate for BUD/S training was only twenty percent. The instructors loved to point that out regularly. Only one of every five would graduate. What was expected of each of us was about to be made clearer.

"Line up, sirs."

And we did. Eight ensigns, two of us from the US Naval Academy, two from their successful Army careers, and four from the fleet, formed a line next to the infamous brass bell, which most of this class would ring, in sad defeat, one day.

The bell sparkled in the sun. Its white braided pull handle attached to the clapper that made a noise that would mark the end of BUD/S training for many. It would be detached from its current display place and put on a truck to follow us around during Hell Week.

"I am Chief Rogers, Gentlemen. You are the leaders of Class 81. I need you to hear what I am going to say very clearly," he growled. "Your future depends on it."

He was a powerful and quiet professional. He wore a khaki short-sleeve uniform. Muscles bulged such that his sleeves seemed too small. His face seemed both serious and amused. He had done this before, and the message he needed us to hear had been given to other officers in other classes. He knew that most of us would not make the cut, but he did not yet know who would fail. On the wall, next to where we stood at attention, was a small wooden plaque commemorating Class 78.

The Class that Was, but wasn't.

Not one member of that class, that started a brief time ago, had finished first phase. Four were rolled back to the next class with one on crutches, and one with an arm in a sling. They would finish with the later class, but there had not been enough left after Hell Week to make a boat crew with their starting class.

"This is the only military training course in the Navy where enlisted instructors will tell officers what to do. We will do it with respect. We will ask you to do everything we ask your classmates to do, plus a little bit more. We will say "Sir" when we do it. But let me be clear about this, if you graduate from this training, I will be telling you, and all my teammates, that I am willing to follow you into our very special kind of combat."

His voice had a deep growl built into it that was both serious and threatening.

Chief Rogers's hard, professional face focused on us menacingly, and his sharply creased khaki uniform was adorned with a gold trident and gold master parachutist's wings that all instructors wore. Between those adornments were five rows of ribbons with four colorful individual ribbons per row. Some ribbons had a "V" device denoting valor in combat. The concept of wearing that same trident one day had crossed all our minds, but it was a very, very long way away now.

Gazing through the Second Phase office window was YN1 Gary Gallagher, one of only five Navy Cross Medal recipients awarded to SEALs so far. To earn this, the nation's second highest combat award, the recipient had to have been nominated for the Medal of Honor. His citation noted caring for, and then carrying, a wounded teammate over six kilometers after a prolonged battle with overwhelming forces, while extracting with their captured enemy. He was waiting to see which of us would be his responsibility if we made it through Hell Week.

"If at any time during this training, my fellow instructors or I determine that we are not willing to follow you into combat, Gentlemen, you will not be here the next day. Am I clear?" he rumbled menacingly.

"Hooyah, Instructor Rogers," we stuttered loudly in reply, without much sincerity.

I felt like wetting my pants. I was scared shitless. I had been challenged before by men that wanted to see me fail. At the Naval Academy, I had led the class in demerits for screwing up in the many, and imaginative, ways I often found. Academy upperclassmen watched me and challenged me to fail. I had succeeded, despite their many and sinister efforts, and graduated, but there were many times in those four years that graduation was brought into serious question.

Now, this well-respected legend in the UDT/SEAL Teams was asking each of us to personally prove to him that we were capable of leading him into combat. We were all incredulous.

I knew how to shoot a rifle and a pistol; I learned how in the Boy Scouts. The two Army officers had yet to see combat, but they had trained with the best the Army had. This was a leap in logic that we could not easily grasp. Rogers had served, fought, and killed in the most demanding of combat situations – behind enemy lines in Vietnam. He had been tested, wounded, and found wanting for nothing. How could we prove our worth to a man like this? My own greatest achievement to date had been to avoid getting kicked out of college for misconduct.

"Dismissed, Gentlemen," he stated with resolve. "Go join your class. They need you with them, and I expect you to lead from the front."

There was a hopeful kindness in his voice, but most of us missed that.

We ran back in the dark early dawn and formed up with the class. For the instructors, PT had been a delightful start to a delightful day. For us it was a first taste of what was to come, and we all wondered where this day would lead us.

After the sixty minutes of exhausting stretches and calisthenics (and our introductory pep talk by Chief Rogers), the sun was beginning to peak over the horizon, and rays of cool sun shone onto the incoming surf crashing only a short distance away from the BUD/s area.

"Class 81, form up for the run," came the next command, and we all rushed to form a four-column semblance of a formation, officers in front, that would depart quickly for destinations along the shore of the Pacific Ocean.

So far, it was a wonderful day. The sun was shining, and the sand was soft, and I was not at sea on the grey monster made of World War II metal held together by rust and paint. I was only responsible for myself. There were more senior officers leading the class, and I felt invisible. This was a relief of significant proportions. To not have to deal with men sentenced to service in the Navy as opposed to jail was a vacation of sorts (military service was sometimes offered to young men by judges, as an alternative to incarceration).

Now I was standing with men of such high caliber that the recent past was just a distant blur. I reveled in the difference, and so did most of the others. We had found a place in the now-shrinking military where we could be proud of our mission and the men we worked with. The underwater demolition teams were jumping into the oceans to rescue astronauts and train sea lions to recover deep lost torpedoes. The Teams were still a secret organization – and rumors suggested they could eat John Wayne and his Green Berets for breakfast!

The run was over, and our daily PT was starting to make us increasingly fit and our muscles stronger and harder. It was time to make a run to the chow hall over one mile away, across the strand, at the Naval amphibious base. We ran in formation, with instructors calling cadence, to a well-earned and copious hot meal. The marines we passed paused to watch us. They had seen this passage of men in formation many times, and they knew our numbers would dwindle each week as training took its toll. There was a quiet pride among us, as none believed we would be the ones missing in future weeks.

The typical Navy-issue burgundy tray slid along the rails with an empty plate and plastic glass filled with iced sodas. We were eyeing the food steaming in stainless trays ahead. We all needed to get as much as the plate could hold. Scrambled eggs in large mounds made way for a biscuit and sausage crumbled into white gravy, with the meat of the day piled alongside. Bacon (and necessary grease) with fried potatoes rounded out the plate. Grapefruit slices in sugar held space in a separate bowl. Toast with butter slid in next to all the rest with multiple strawberry jam individual serving containers. This would be our first trip through the line today. There would be one more for lunch. It probably tasted good, and I remember a feeling of great satisfaction when my stomach registered full, but quantity mattered, and a full stomach was the goal. Sometimes food choices were made based on caloric content, or solid verses liquid to ensure prompt passage, effective elimination, and subsequent tank refills. It became more and more important to learn what fuel worked best.

At 5 foot 8, I weighed a comfortable 155 pounds and had a touch of fat layered beneath my skin that I could pinch if I wanted. This fat would soon be replaced by an increasing muscle mass as it was burned for fuel. I felt fit, as I had been running and swimming and doing calisthenics every day. I was not fit *enough*.

In fact, *fit* was soon to be redefined in ways that would surprise us all – by repeated events consisting of prolonged pre-dawn physical training and long late-night ocean swims in colder-than-expected salt water, by obstacle courses, and by grueling long-distance runs. Most of us had played high school and college sports and had been coached by professionals who expected much of us, but nothing had prepared us for what was ahead. Today was a kind and gentle day comparatively. We all knew already that calories were essential to survival. Many would pack on muscle weight as training progressed. I would eventually weigh 175 pounds without a hint of fat to pinch.

We all noticed the changes. Run times targets decreased from early expectations of four miles in thirty-two minutes to the same distance in under thirty minutes, and the boots and sand were so much a part of the effort that we seldom had to think about it. Pull-ups and dips (a new exercise on parallel bars needed for the obstacle course) became enjoyable. Seaman Apprentice McNabb, our junior class member and a hardened farm boy, would show off at times by doing his pull-ups *s l o w l y*. That made them much harder, and impressed the instructors appropriately, since pull-ups were never actually fun.

It was still fun and exciting to earn a Navy paycheck, to workout daily, and try to earn a place alongside the men we had all seen on the walls of the building where we had reported for duty. I personally pictured myself in the ocean with a knife on my side, covered with grease for warmth like the World War II frogmen I had learned about. I had visions of leading men with amazing skills in combat. The Naval Academy had taught me of great battles and great men. I just wanted to be a part of recent history. Vietnam was over now, but it was still a very real part of the nation's recent memories. Our instructors wore awards that most had only read about. It was humbling and a bit scary to think that we might be asked to work alongside such men.

Today it was all about preparation. Prepare for the next event. Take each day as a personal test of ability, stamina, and commitment. Most of us were excited with each new day, and we were in training with men equally driven to succeed. Thoughts of swimming, diving, parachuting, blowing up obstacles underwater, patrolling through enemy-infested jungles holding advanced weapons, and proving that we could be a part of this fraternity of warriors were things we *all* thought about but were not confident enough to express out loud.

Now was a time of testing. Now was a time to prove we belonged, one day at a time.

"OK Gents, we are going to play a game."

There was an ominous smile on the face of the instructor. Breakfast was burning up fast in our bellies, and we were warm from the run back to the training area. It was the next evolution in another long day of evolutions.

"I want you to form a line and begin the push-up challenge. Line up and do one push-up, then run to the other end of the grinder and do two push-ups, then come back and do three. Keep going until you cannot do another. When you fail, you may hit the surf."

This was fun. We smiled at the comparatively simple task and began in earnest. Instructors enjoyed the game as they wandered end to end declaring the losers, who ran to the Pacific Ocean a hundred yards away and got wet. The line of wet spectators grew as the number reached 20, then 21, then 22. The cumulative number of push-ups was growing, and only two men remained. We cheered them on. Bobby McNabb and Don Sayre were push-up animals. They went on and on and on, like machines. The instructors waited for the inevitable final failure to declare a winner. Bobby and Don just smiled at each other, sweat rolling off their noses, as the instructors began to realize that the expected end was not soon in sight. These men had muscles that would not tire any time soon. We would see this over and over during training in the months to come. They knew no physical limits it seemed. We were all having fun watching the event go on as the sun warmed our wet clothes. There was no jealousy about their God-given, vigorous, work-developed strength – there was just hope that they would be where we needed them if we needed help. We were a team, and we celebrated each other's successes most of the time.

Seaman Apprentice Bob McNabb was a mature teenager at eighteen. He was fit, muscular, and a leader in everything he did. He had a laugh and sense of humor that never stopped. People always did what he asked of them in just about any situation. They had always done it, and he was often confused by their trust in him. He was married to the love of his life, and she was his strength and best friend. He called her his "shipmate" which combined his love and his friendship into a term his civilian and private life partner could appreciate. His life away from her was often with his shipmates from the fleet, or now his shipmates at BUD/S. She liked knowing that she was at least as important as the men that took him away from her.

Seaman Don Sayre was nineteen and had been adopted by an older couple. They had been caring for a young pregnant girl whose boyfriend had deserted her. When she announced being unable to handle a child, Don was born and adopted into the older couple's family. He grew up poor and had worked as an assistant manager at the ice rink where he played hockey. The money he earned helped his mother and adopted family buy necessities. The Catholic Church had paid for his food and books at school, and he had almost been denied graduation if he had missed one more day of school due to work. He wore hand-me-down clothes that always smelled of his chain-smoking parent's cigarette smoke. He had earned a swimming scholarship to Indiana State University plus three other colleges as a super star on the school swim team. He held the school records in freestyle and butterfly events. His grades were good, and he liked to swim. He was 6 feet 1 and weighed 172. He was lean and handsome, but life looked much better elsewhere, so he had joined the Navy to become a SEAL.

But he went to the fleet first. Prior to training orders, he had finished a boring and demeaning four months chipping paint and polishing brass on one of the few remaining post–World War II cruisers, the USS *Newport News* (CA-148). Its rust dated back to her launch in March 1948. He had lived in the pitch-black bowels of an all-steel compartment, hidden below the ship's waterline. His rack was a standard, hanging canvas fold-up bed with a thin used mattress where the smells and noises of too many others lingered all around him. It was a reprieve from this jail type lodging when his orders came, launching him like a bottle rocket to Coronado, California, where he happily accepted a barracks bunk in a real room with real sunlight.

Don had been seven years old when his elderly adopted father died, and male role models were hard to come by after that. He could run, and he could swim, and he could drink beer with the best. He played hockey hard and fast. His neighbor's SEAL stories had given him a seemingly exciting way out of his harder-than-necessary life. If he could get to training, it was unimaginable to him that he would fail. Failure would send him back to the hell he had lived, and that would not be acceptable under any circumstances. If he had stayed where he had grown up, jail time was most likely in his future.

As it turned out, the shipboard time was well spent. It showed him that the difficulties he knew at home were not the only type of shit he could step in. A ship at sea operated twenty-four hours a day, and every hour was regimented.

"Enough," announced the instructor who inwardly smiled at the achievements of our two strongest men. "We do not have enough time to declare a winner, so you both win. Take a break, you two, while your classmates run the obstacle course."

We left together for the short run to the now familiar obstacle course while Bobby and Don followed at a slower jog, to watch.

The obstacle course was a test of strength and agility. It was timed, and failure to meet the fifteen-minute minimum time was common, but still unacceptable. We would all beat the required time eventually, and it would become an event to master and brag about – but now it was a small horror. Set entirely in soft sand, there were monkey bars to hand walk across, parallel bars to wobble or hop along with straight arms supporting the body, balance beams to run across, rope walls to scramble up, walls to climb that tilted towards you, three-story towers that were far enough apart that you had to jump up to grab each level, twenty-foot-high ladders that led to long ropes to slide down, and barbed wire to crawl under. It took twenty or more minutes to make it through the entire course in the beginning, but that would soon be a failing time. Technique and strength would develop together, or failure would follow.

Bobby and Don did not *have* to sweat this event today, but they did. They had earned a small break, but that was not how we had discussed our future. We would succeed or fail together.

"Bobby, what is our next event after the O course?" asked Don as they walked toward the class now gathering into formation.

"I think it's the fucking golf course run, and I hate that run. It is just a bit too far for my Adonis-like body to endure," he smiled as he wiped away sweat and tucked his T-shirt into his pants.

"Do we sit this out then, and be better at the run later? What will the instructors think of that choice? How is that teamwork? I think we should run the course anyway?" he rambled in one long thought process.

"Aw damn, I knew you were going to say something like that. Let's get in formation and impress them all. But look out, I think I might just try and trip you on the run if you try to pass me again."

We all knew Hell Week was coming fast, and we would need each other to finish. Bobby and Don lined up with the rest to meet the challenge of the O-course. Don was still feeling invincible, as always. His belief in himself would continue to serve him well.

The instructors noticed, and smiled. Seaman Bobby McNabb would be chosen by the instructors, at graduation, to be our Honor Man. Of the eleven that would walk across the podium at graduation, one would be declared as the best of the lot. Bobby would be that man, and he would justify that honor many times over as the months careened by. He would further justify that recognition in the team for years to follow. We would all be proud to say he began his career with our class.

But this morning's obstacle course was going to be very different for all. Petty Officer First Class Mike Thornton was reporting for training as our instructor. Everyone knew he was coming. ENS Muggs remembered having seen him in the hallway when he had reported in, and we all had heard the slightly unbelievable story of how he had saved his officer and squad on a mission deep behind enemy lines in Vietnam. That officer was severely wounded, but made it back alive due to Mike's extraordinary bravery, leadership, and superhuman willpower. What made it historically extraordinary was that the officer he saved had already earned the Medal of Honor for a previous mission.

He was intimidating to look at. He was also burdened for life with being known everywhere he went because of the Medal of Honor on his dress uniform.

Instructor Thornton was a large man with a serious face. He had thick, dark hair and muscles on top of his muscles. He had carried the burdensome M60 machine gun in Vietnam like it were a toy. He was unnerving, to say the least.

I would be introduced to Mike up close and personal very soon.

The obstacle course was becoming fun now. We were getting better at the techniques needed to pull, slide, crawl, and jump over and under the various challenges in the soft sand. Petty Officer Frank Winget, having joined us from a previous class, held the O-course record, and helped us all with technique.

I was happily in the middle of the crowd and was happy with my time, as I stood with the finishers covered with sweat and sand. So I began to tuck my T-shirt into my pants, brush off the sand, and prepare for the coming three-mile run around the amphibious base.

Unfortunately for me, Instructor Joe Tyvdik, a lean, strong willow of a man was watching over all. He caught a flash of navy blue between the buttons of my BDU uniform pants and realized that I had very likely chosen to violate the rule to not wear underwear during training. This rule made sense to avoid the inevitable chaffing and possible infections that came from clothing and sand mixing in the groin area.

I knew the rule, and I understood the reasoning behind it, but we were going on a long run after the O-course, and I felt better running with some support, so I made a personal decision that I was sure no one cared about except me.

Oops.

"ENS Adams," he crooned with an evil smile, as he sauntered dangerously towards me.

"What have we here?" he continued as he reached for my groin area to display the blue and gold Naval Academy issue, Speedo bathing suit I was hiding under my uniform.

My mind was racing. I was a master of excuses. I could invent reasons for anything out of thin air with no notice. But as he reached for my groin, and I anticipated the possible trouble I was in, my mind froze. Nothing came to me. I needed to divert attention away from me.

So I brushed Instructor Tyvdik's hand away and playfully stated in mock horror, "Instructor Tyvdik, get your hand away from there. What are you, some kind of a faggot?"

I took this chance in a moment of panic. It was the best I could come up with at the time. It was a serious gamble made worse by being unaware of my surroundings at the time. I was smiling in desperation that the timing and humor was right and was rewarded with a surprised smile as he stepped back. It looked like I might just get away with it.

Only a few feet away, however, was another instructor, unaware of the flash of blue in my pants or *why* we were having this animated discussion, and he had heard my comment.

This was as Instructor Mike Thornton trotted out toward the O-course for his first event as our newest instructor. Seeing a significant opportunity for entertainment and pain, the other instructor waited until Mike grew close. and then screeched for all to hear.

"Mike, that damn officer just called Instructor Tyvdik a faggot!"

We all froze, as a dark cloud came over Mike's face, while he slowed to a trot and pulled up right in front of me. I was petrified. This was not going anywhere near where I had hoped. Situational awareness had failed me.

He glanced at my name tag and gold collar bars of an ensign and screamed, "Drop for twenty, you filthy maggot!"

As I fell to leaning rest, he fell with me, and crammed his nose against my forehead as we moved together up and down in quick push-ups.

"Do you want to call *me* a faggot, Mr. Adams?" he screamed, as we pushed up and down, fused together at my forehead.

"If you even *think* about it, I will bite your head off, and shit in the hole."

His spittle was spraying in my face, and I could feel the heat from his own red face. The other instructors and students were moving quietly and quickly out of range. I knew the threat was not physically possible, but damn if I didn't envision him doing just that.

"No, Instructor Thornton," was all I could muster in return. The rest of the class was still coming in from the last barbed-wire crawl obstacle on the O-course, and whispers were informing them of my predicament as they assembled to brush off and redo their uniforms.

"Get your ass up and get ready to run that O-course again, you filthy scum bucket. I want you to run that obstacle course again, right now. And I want you to run it backwards. Now go, and do not even consider not making a passing time."

I took off immediately for the last barbed wire obstacle, as another class-mate was coming through the correct way. I tried to think about how I was going to accomplish this task. I would have to climb up the 200-foot rope of the Slide-for-Life obstacle that we usually slid *down*, and I had never seen that done before. Other seemingly insurmountable problems lay ahead, but I was running on adrenalin, and was somewhat relieved to be on my own, away from a perceived certain death that had threatened me moments ago.

The class was formed up and ready to go when I crawled back to the original starting line, filthy and exhausted. Blood leaked down one elbow and dripped off my left hand from where the wooden edge of one obstacle had shaved off a chunk of skin. I was unaware.

"Mr. Adams, you are an officer, a *leader*. Get to the front of the formation and lead this run. Go!" he bellowed, as he pushed me forward, while I tried to catch my breath.

"Double-time march," came the order, and the class leaped ahead on our planned three-mile run. The class had rested well while I had burned the oxygen from my muscles on the O-course. Now I was gasping to stay in front while my mind tried to assess the situation. It was grim.

After five minutes of running, we were entering the golf course area, and Thornton pulled me out of formation and ordered me to "hit the bay." Glorietta Bay lined the edge of the golf course, and I sprinted towards the nearest wetness where I encountered cattails, and mud, and shallow water. I splashed into the wetness and rolled to get wet all over while the class trotted on. My boots filled with water.

"Catch up with your class Mr. Officer, you are supposed to be a leader," shouted Mike as he propelled me towards the class. I sprinted with all I had and made it to the main group. If it were not for the power of adrenalin, I would not have made it. I slipped into the formation middle, and asked those around me to hide me.

"Guys, help me here. Hide me," I panted as I wriggled into the middle.

"Oh, Lordy," I heard whispered behind me.

They moved away. There was a hole in the middle of the formation with me in it. I was a dead man, and they all knew it. So much for teamwork today.

Five minutes further on, Mike had fallen back to harass some of the stragglers that were not keeping up, when he realized I was not back there. He saw a large puddle coming up on the dirt road ahead, came alongside the main group, and ordered us all to drop for push-ups in the muddy water.

"Mr. Adams, are you in there?" he queried.

"Yes, Instructor," I muttered from the middle of the now wet and muddy crowd, paused in leaning rest positions.

"I need you to head on back to the compound, and save us all a lot of pain and suffering. Ring the bell now so we can get on with training. You sir, are not going to make it. Today is your last day here. I promise you that, so take off now. Ring the fucking bell."

I was stunned. "How did this happen? It was just a bathing suit worn to protect me."

I looked up at this giant of a man, looked him dead in the eye, and whispered the words "No way."

He read my lips and seemingly liked what I had mouthed at him.

"Get up all, and resume the run. Adams drop for twenty more," he ordered, and I stayed in the mud pushing out twenty more as the class moved on, grateful to be rid of me. I finished and took off, as fast as my spent lungs could handle, towards the main group a hundred yards ahead. Some stragglers caught Mike's eye and he took off after them. Again, I clawed my way into the main group of runners. I was on pure jet drive now and had no idea what to do, so I hung on.

The run ended back at the grinder, and only half the class was still in formation. The rest were spread out along the course being urged and threatened by the other instructors. We were ordered to stay in formation and march around the grinder as the rest of the class straggled in.

Instructor Thornton came in next and stationed himself at the chain link fence gate entrance watching the class come in. He was looking for me, sure that I must be huffing and puffing back in the rear. When the last few had come in, he looked around and asked another instructor where I was.

"He's over there with the main group. He finished with the pack."

"No fucking way!? Mr. Adams, get over here and give me twenty push-ups again. Did you finish that run with the main group?"

"Yes, Instructor Thornton," I panted as respectfully as I could.

"Well you just wasted your time and effort, since this is the last day of training for you. Get your ass down to the ocean, get wet, and roll yourself in the sand until every nook and crack of your body is covered. You will look like a sugar cookie when you get back here. Go!"

Sugar cookie was the term used to describe a wet *tadpole* covered with sand. To achieve this uncomfortable state, a trainee had to get wet all over by leaping into the surf, run to the dry edge of the beach, remove helmet, and then roll over and sideways until the clothes, skin, hair, ears and eyes were coated in sand. Thus, we resembled a human sugar cookie.

As I ran to the ocean, the rest of the class was ordered back to the barracks to change into dry clothing for the subsequent classroom event. When I got back they were gone. I was wet and carefully covered with sand, and held an extra handful to put on my head in case the helmet had rubbed some off. I already had sand in my mouth and ears in case he checked there. As I approached, I lifted my helmet and placed the sand under it. Sand was everywhere and falling from under my helmet.

"God damn it, Mr. Adams, did you just brush sand off your head?!" he shrilled, as if astonished. "I told you to have sand everywhere. Now go back and do it again *correctly*," he ordered with emphasis.

He smiled professionally as I moved away stuttering my disbelief. He knew what I had done and why. He had done it himself when he was in training, but I was destined to fail today, if he had his way.

There was no response that would work in this situation, and I could not read his face, so I about-faced and headed back to the ocean. Sugar cookie he wanted, and sugar cookie he would get. The few minutes each way gave me pause to think of a way out of this situation. I had clearly crossed a line that I did not know was there, and now I was facing an angry nightmare wearing the Medal of Honor. I decided to go on. I could imagine no way out. I had no other choice. I believed it would end eventually, at least I hoped so.

Push-ups, sand dune climbs, flutter kicks, sprints to the ocean and back, threats, screams and anger, followed me for the next few hours. My arms were shaking, and my legs burned, and the ocean's icy frostiness was feeling therapeutic when I was immersed in it time after time.

The class was obliquely aware that they had lost an officer as Thornton's voice filtered into the class from behind the closed door. He had promised to run me out of training, and they were sitting as silent witnesses to this expected, inevitable event.

It was 1130 and the blood on my hand had long since dried. We had started the O-course at 0800, and I was in a leaning rest position, following a sprint along the tops of the undulating soft sand dunes, a dip in the ocean, and another roll in the sand. Instructor Thornton was once again entreating me to quit because what was going on was going to continue until I did so. I endured. It was the only hope I had. I spoke when spoken to, and did the best I could to do as ordered.

I was in the leaning rest position again, back at the PT area. The water was pooling under me, and both my arms and legs were shaking with a mind of their own. I was looking straight down, and I was devoid of thought. I was in pure survival mode.

"OK mister, we are done here. Go join your class," stated my tormentor firmly and officially, and he walked away.

I was left alone, confused and exhausted as I watched my dedicated tormentor just walk away. My mind was processing what had just been said. I struggled up, looked around confused, spit grit out of my mouth, stood up unsteadily, and stumbled towards the nearby classroom filled with clean dry classmates. The teacher was at the board going over the lesson, and he paused when I opened the door and stumbled to an open desk.

ENS Muggs was sitting just behind me and was watching me carefully. Nothing was said. I was a dead man walking, but returned from the grave. So, the instructor resumed his lesson, and I began to shake. Sand fluttered to the clean floor below me and my boots oozed salt water into puddles around me. I heard nothing, and I felt abused, confused, and angry. I had been thinking for the last few hours that my small crime did not justify this punishment. I knew that to some extent Instructor Thornton *had* to do what he was doing as both a new and famous instructor, and because he did not know me yet. Still I had been unable to think of a way to stop what was happening, except to endure. The longer it had gone on, the more unnecessary it had felt. I was confused. I had been harassed before at the Naval Academy by upperclassmen who stated they wanted me to leave, but there seemed more at stake now. To fail now, to *not* endure, would end everything before I had a chance to show what I could do.

My face turned red, and the shaking got worse as I contemplated the events of the past few hours. I felt like a piece of horse dung dropped onto the field of sweet grass surrounding me. I did not know what to do now. What waited for me next?

"Excuse us please, Instructor?" asked ENS Muggs, a fellow Naval Academy graduate, as he stood up, gently grabbed my arm, and led me outside the room. This was an unusual move by a trainee, but the instructor saw that this was an unusual situation, so he nodded concurrence.

We moved together outside with my new protector supporting me physically. "Bob, you did it. You survived. Calm down and take a few deep breaths."

We walked slowly back and forth on the sidewalk area, and I regained a measure of calm. Adrenalin was all I had been running on, and now it seemed like I had very little left.

"That was uncalled for," I muttered.

John agreed, but it was what it was. The purpose was not yet revealed. Eventually, after a few walks back and forth, as calm returned, and the reality of survival sunk in, I was escorted back to the class. I did not hear the instructor. I was lost in my musings. My biggest worry was that the test was not complete. What if I had made a fatal mistake? Could I go through all that again, and again?

The next morning at 0430, we again gathered on the grinder in our assigned positions for morning PT. I had just assumed my front row spot when I was summoned.

"ENS Adams, get your ass over here, and give me twenty-five," growled Mike Thornton.

Behind me PT began, and the whole class began their first set of jumping jack exercises. A few wondered if they would ever see me again. I began to think about yesterday.

As I finished the push-ups and held still in the leaning rest position, I looked up, in fear, for the next command.

Mike Thornton was seated on a platform over me, legs crossed, and watching carefully.

"So, Mr. Adams, do you remember yesterday when I told you I was going to run you out of training?"

"Yes, Instructor," I replied as my mind tried to digest the horror of that statement. We had months and months of training ahead, and if I had to do yesterday again today, and every day, there was no chance I would survive.

"Well, I changed my mind. You did well yesterday. I am not going to run you out. As a matter of fact, I am going to make sure you graduate," he stated calmly and with conviction.

I was speechless, and I felt the muscles in my back and legs relax. I almost wet myself.

"But let me be clear about one thing, if you screw up, you will answer to me, and the penalty will be severe. So when you graduate, and you *will* graduate, there will be no question in your mind that you, *sir*, have been through training."

Angels were singing above. The sun was peaking above the horizon just for me. A warm relief flooded over me.

"Hooyah, Instructor Thornton." I replied, and risked a small smile.

I think I saw him smile also when he turned away.

"You are never a loser until you quit trying."
—Mike Ditka

Chapter 6
First Phase learning

The California sun reflected brightly off the flat Pacific Ocean. PT, run, and breakfast were memories as we lined up for log PT to start our day. We still had all eight officers, but for reasons known only to them, six more men had rung the bell three times, and left us. We were now a class of fifty-six and this was only our first week of real training. A few of the men who quit did so at night. They slipped out of the barracks and walked to the bell and rang it softly three times. They then presented to the duty officer who arranged for their prompt departure. Their personal effects disappeared also. Questions of why they quit were never answered.

Sometimes we would hear the bell ring during the day and look around to find one boat crew lamenting the loss of a member as the now alone swim buddy was left to be reassigned. We all had swim buddies, and we tried to encourage and support each other. When a swim buddy quit, both men were affected. The team leaders would quickly jump in and support the man left behind.

"You did great trying to help him. We all did," encouraged RM3 Tom Valentine the current boat crew leader. "He made a choice, and he must live with it. We, however, will go on, and you will be here at the end with the rest of us."

"I still feel like I could have done more. He started talking about quitting this morning, and I thought I had him convinced to stay. All he had was a pulled muscle in his back from log PT yesterday. We would have helped him today, got him to sick call, and he would have done fine. Shit Tommy, he kicked my ass on the four-mile run last Friday," he noted with despair.

"I know. I don't understand either, but let's focus on today and move on."

"Instructor, I need a new swim buddy assignment for Petty Officer Banton please," stated Valentine softly as he moved to the nearest instructor's blue and gold shirt.

MM3 Dave Banton was 5 foot 10 and weighed a thin 117 pounds when he had arrived at pre-training. The regular food and daily workouts had packed on some real muscle. He now weighed 147 pounds, and had no fat at all visible.

Dave had wanted to go to BUD/S soon after enlisting, but was directed to the fleet for one year before being allowed to apply. He was good with machines, so he went to machinist mate school. That led to the USS *Buchannan* (DDG-14) where he served as a *snipe* (enlisted engineering staff) in the overwhelmingly hot bowels of the engine rooms. He would look back on his three summer months in the Indian Ocean as an endurance test opposite to what he faced now. The heat had been oppressive and required those on watch to stand directly under the huge overhead vents to simply breathe, while watching the engine gauges.

Luckily for Dave, there was a new warrant officer SEAL assigned to his ship. WO Phillip "Moki" Martin had already been in the Teams for ten years and was known for his triathlon accomplishments and his heroism in Vietnam. WO Martin took Dave under his wing and had him running around the ship and working out in the engine room. It had been both athletically valuable and career motivating.

Banton was reassigned to a new swim buddy.

"Stick with me, buddy. I will help you, if you will help me. There is no way I am ever going back to the ship I came from," he told his new compadre. "I will die here in the mud or sand first." They both smiled at the thought.

Days were long, and every minute was filled with running, swimming, PT, strength exercises, obstacle courses, rubber boat drills in the surf, and any other event that would build us up as we were being prepared for what was to come. It was like being in an Olympic training center, except our trainers were not that encouraging. Mostly, they challenged us to fail. They criticized and encouraged with the same enthusiasm. At the same time, they watched, they discussed, and they reported what they saw.

Last week had cost us two classmates. We had been learning in the daytime how to land our rubber boats onto the monstrous rocks of the jetty in front of the Hotel del Coronado. The waves had been high that day, and the rocks were wet and slippery. We had been briefed on what to do.

The briefing had consisted of a review of all previous day and night surf passage events we had practiced over the last two weeks. It reviewed the types of waves we had encountered and which methods had worked best when the waves were spilling or crunching, and how wind and angles of the waves to the beach affected boat performance. It reviewed the dump boat drill procedures and the use of handles and ropes used to right the swamped boat.

Finally, we took all this background information and applied it to the event ahead where the landing area was strewn with hippopotamus sized slippery rocks, stacked together as a water break; this was in front of the hotel and civilian beach area. These nasty, intimidating obstacles had been blasted from the side of a cliff somewhere and transported to the site to act as a protective barrier against the pounding surf. BUD/S instructors quickly realized the intimidation value of these sharp-edged monsters and added a rock portage event to training and Hell Week. The briefing itself was a bit discomforting, but we were told that our training should pay off. Some were more confident than others, since a few of our officers and senior enlisted classmates had yet to perfect steering a boat in rough surf.

We had thought it through in our minds, but the actual intimidating process would require timing by the coxswain and teamwork by the paddlers. The goal was to land the boat, wearing heavy kapok lifejackets, in heavy surf, onto the rocks. We were to then exit the boat by pairs, maintain control of the 300-pound IBS (inflatable boat, small), and drag it onto and *over* the slippery rocks. The chance for injury was high and ever present.

Classroom time had taught us about the types of waves we would be asked to swim and paddle through. We had learned all about waves. There were three basic types. Spilling, surging and plunging (also called "crunchers") waves were studied and observed in the classroom and at the beach. The tide, wind, and bottom slope (or gradient) affected the type of waves we would deal with when swimming out or paddling through the surf. Spilling and surging waves were a gas to ride in on as they pushed the boats along like toys. We simply had to keep the boat facing forward. The coxswain in the back gave steerage with his paddle acting like a rear rudder. He also gave commands to the port and starboard paddlers.

If we were going in or out of the surf, the larger plunging waves were difficult to negotiate, and timing was imperative. If you were caught in the rising inside curvature of a "cruncher" then the wave would break right on top of the boat and push it down and backwards towards the shore. It would be impossible to paddle through this type of wave if the timing was wrong. The result would be bodies and boat thrown about and washed ignominiously back to the shore. Often the boat would flip over. This would be disorienting, and swim buddies were often separated.

Losing your swim buddy came with harsh penalties, including being tied together by a long heavy ship's rope, four inches in diameter; it was heavy and called attention to all that this pair had failed to watch out for each other. This was a cardinal sin, as would be taught over and over in every setting we would train in. Watch out for your swim buddy, and he will watch out for you. Survival depended on it. Swim pair assignments changed regularly as our numbers dwindled, and boat crews were shuffled to ensure at least one officer and one senior enlisted per boat crew.

Today, the waves were six-foot crunchers, and every boat had tried and failed at least once to make it out to the calmer water past the breaking waves. This was another daytime practice for a coming pitch-black nighttime event. Everyone was now soaked and wrapped in soggy, bulky kapok lifejackets.

"OK, King Neptune, god of the sea, give it your best shot," demanded Winget. "I have told you before, and I'm telling you now, that I am not afraid of you. Your ocean is my ocean too, and I will not let you get the best of me."

His crew members smiled.

This was a mental exercise he enjoyed. He had chosen this way to deal with the fear that had messed heavily with his mind the last time he was in training. The waves were loud and hissing, and the crash was palpable as the sound of the waves assaulted boat, paddle, and paddler. When an IBS got caught in the powerful rush of water, it could flip, or slide sideways, or fill with water. Often, it would trap someone underneath it, and paddles would fly up into the air, where teeth were at risk.

Not today. Winget was sitting up front in the so-called number-one starboard position. His boat made it out through the surf as a last breaking wave flowed over them. They were paddling as hard as they could to keep the bow pointing into the waves, and it broke right on top of him as both he and the other port number-one paddler reached forward and pulled with all their might. In the back, ENS Albracht was using his powerful wrestler's arms to push and pull the stern of the boat with his paddle, used as a mobile rudder, to keep it pointing straight ahead.

"Ha! Neptune, I win again, and I will keep fighting what you send my way," screamed Winget, with a satisfied grin as he spit the mouthful of salty sea back where it came from.

Frank had grown up in central Florida where the word poor was insufficient to describe the life his family was stuck in. He was tall and skinny. He did not scare anyone, but he was as tough as life had made him. The Navy offered him a job and great food, and he gained weight and grew an inch more at boot camp. He loved the clean white uniforms and shiny brass. But after quitting early during a past Hell Week, he had been assigned to the USS *Anchorage* (LSD-36) based across the water in San Diego, California.

The *Anchorage* had made a once in a lifetime cruise to Anchorage, Alaska, for a goodwill visit the previous year with Frank on board. He remembered it well. This LSD (Landing Ship Dock) was launched in March 1969, so it was relatively new when he had arrived there. It would earn 6 battle stars in its Vietnam service, and in later years be used as a target, and sunk by a USS *Bremerton* (SSN-698) torpedo, for training purposes, in July 2010.

But much to Frank's surprise, on board the ship was a UDT-12 platoon of "rootin-tootin" frogmen. Life was good for frogmen on an amphibious ship. They worked out daily and even had suntan time built into their workday schedules. Two of the platoon members were his previous classmates from Class 72. Now Frank was a good shipboard sailor and had been promoted since he had left training, but in his mind, all he could think of was how his former classmates saw him as a loser. It was the psychological low point of his life at the time. Today was different, however. He was back, and he would not let Neptune or *anyone* stop him now.

Each crew performed the rock portage preparation event for most of the morning under the watchful eyes of instructors standing on the rocks, yelling commands and advice. We were all beaten and bruised to some extent, but before this training event was over, just the thought of doing it again – in the *dark* – cost us two more men.

One of the boat crews had landed on the rocks hard as the wave they were riding rose up and slammed them into a group of large slick monster boulders. When the first two paddlers jumped out, holding onto the front bowline as ordered, the boat surged back with the receding wave and pulled them both together and downward. The water rushed away with the boat, and exposed only bare rock to cushion their falls.

Smack... thud... crack!

The two men hit the rocks, bounced face first into them, and rolled into the sea. Blood poured from the bent and likely broken nose of one man as his swim buddy tried to catch his balance on the rock under him. He still shared a grip on the bowline. His foot slipped between two rocks and lodged there firmly. As he twisted to pull free, the boat with its entire weight and five other men on board surged forward with the next wave. It caught them both full on the body, and back they went with the boat now surging on *top* of them. One ankle snapped immediately as the immense weight pushed him free. The pain was intense and disorienting, so he dropped the line and curled into a fetal position to allow the kapok lifejacket to act as a bobber and cushion, as he held his breath waiting to surface again.

Just next to him, his swim buddy heard his fiberglass helmet hit the rock behind him, and then a blast of stars flooded his vision as his head made contact. There was another pain in the back of his head that equaled the pain in his gushing nose. He allowed the retreating IBS to pull him off the rocks and into the icy sea. He let go once he was floating free and felt carefully behind his skull where the pain was. There was a flap of scalp tissue in his hand that did not seem connected to anything.

Oh no, I am hurt bad, he thought as he held the skin flat to his scalp, dropped his paddle and bowline, and kicked towards shore.

A corpsman saw him coming with a face covered with blood. He had been stabilizing the broken ankle of his swim buddy, but now he launched himself into the surf to help pull his newest charge free of the chaos.

"You look like there is blood everywhere. Are you OK? What happened?" stuttered his shivering buddy laying on the beach with a board lashed to his ankle.

"I have no idea," responded his friend, but I think a rock ripped my scalp off after it broke my nose. Seriously, this is just plain stupid, and I am out of here."

"You mean you are quitting? Even before Hell Week?

"God damn right I am," he said with salt water soaked conviction.

"Well then, I am quitting with you. I heard my bones break, and I am not going to wait around to heal just to do this again. I'm done too." And they both flopped back on the wet sand and let the corpsman do his work.

Following the rock portage training, the boats were paddled back to the center, with more capsized boats washing up on shore, followed by push-ups in the surf zone. Finally, with the sun now high overhead and the wind slowing, we were ordered back, double-time, to the grinder.

We were short two more classmates.

The lunch run was next, and boats were stowed with the paddles and kapoks for future use. Run, eat, and run back again. It was one and one-half miles each way. That was the lunch break.

The next event of the day was the infamous and unpleasant log PT. The run had settled our food a bit. Now each boat crew was assigned a large, heavy log to use in the coming exercise series. It was designed to teach teamwork. Each crew member would share a space on the log as we were ordered to lift them to overhead push-ups, do sit-ups with them in our laps, push them up the slanted beach with our feet, and lift, roll, push, or pull them wherever we were directed. It was exhausting.

As we progressed through this team practice with heavy telephone poles, two instructors paused between yells for "more teamwork" to admire how well ENS Holloway and his team were doing. Holloway was our biggest, most powerful, and most accomplished trainee. No one expected him to quit, ever. His team was performing well with his leadership and strength. Once again, they had won the race pushing their log up and down the sand dunes with their feet. They were all exhausted, but smiling as they had earned a brief rest while the other teams ran to the water to get wet again.

"It pays to be a winner."

As their wet classmates raced back to resume the competition with logs, Holloway pumped up his team with encouragement again. They were up and ready with the log at their feet when the last man raced up to their log.

"Up logs, right shoulder," ordered the instructor, and Holloway's team whipped their monster burden up effortlessly.

"Double-time to the obstacle course *now*," came the next command.

As his team moved out, he chose the rear position so he could direct their progress. They were in the lead as the point man led the way. Unseen by him, the lead man chose the shortest route over some wooden log barriers in the sand. These logs barriers were used to mark boundaries of different training areas. They were mostly old sticky telephone poles cut and laid flat in diverse designs. All six men in front stumbled to avoid the sandy, slippery obstacles and stay in the lead. ENS Holloway could feel his log-wielding team starting to wobble, but could not see the reason why. He stepped quickly forward, as the log surged forward with his men and discovered a round log sticking up fourteen inches above the sand with other telephone poles, laid flat, stretching away at 90-degree angles. His boot slipped on the sand-covered wooden slickness, and the entire weight of his body and log pushed down on his right leg as it twisted uncontrollably. He heard a loud *pop* and went down in severe pain without a yell. He was immediately aware that he had a major issue to deal with, and he knew also that he would not be graduating with this class. It was going to take a little longer.

His right leg was broken at the fibula, and the ankle tendons were torn. It was already turning colors, and swelling, when the instructor got there. Our second most senior officer was now gone. He would heal, and be rolled back to a later class, but we were down to seven officers now.

"Link arms and march your lazy tadpole butts into the surf zone Class 81," directed Instructor Frisk.

We had failed again at the O-course test, with less than half the class obtaining a passing time. This was our second trip to the water for "surf appreciation." The class linked arms and walked in a wavy line towards the one-foot spilling waves that were hitting the Coronado beach at a fifteen-degree angle from the south. Once we were knee deep the next command came.

"Take a seat," and the line of men dropped together into the surrounding froth. To understand this situation, it is worth a review of basic physiology. As soon as boots fill with icy water, small blood vessels contract to prevent blood flow and subsequent loss of stored body heat. This moment of autonomic response sends waves of stinging shock up the legs. Now, in preparation for further heat conservation, testicles start to retreat. They are pulled into the groin by the cremaster muscles. This cremasteric response was dramatic as we dropped into the water to our waist. We had all determined by now that slow is bad, and quick is better. Just get it over with, and get wet and cold all at once. This way all the surface and extremity vessels can go into their protection mode simultaneously.

The body cannot easily ready itself for cold insults. When it happens, the automatic protection mechanisms kick in quickly. The body's control centers are programmed to protect vital internal organs. As core body temperatures drop, even internal organs must shunt blood to the most needed areas. We would all learn later that, sometimes, to keep the heart beating, the brain itself would be deprived of nutrient blood. Basic functions, including thought and memory, would be dulled. Bowels would slow down, urine output would decrease, and even vision would be confused by real inputs viewed as hallucinations.

After six weeks of daily training with running, swimming, boat paddling and surf passage, obstacle course, and whistle drills, we were fit and ready to begin. The whistle drills were designed to make us ready for one single event in the coming week.

"So Solly Day" was going to be a day of demolition exploding all around us on the beach and water. It was intended to find out if there were any among us that would panic under fire. One whistle tweet meant "Hit the deck!" and on command, we would all drop to the ground, cover our heads with our arms, and open our mouths in anticipation of a blast wave. The second double tweet would be sounded somewhere, and we would begin a low crawl towards the sound. Once we were all grouped together at the feet of the whistle blower, to the satisfaction of all watching, a triple tweet would sound, and we would recover to our original standing positions, waiting for the process to repeat. Sometimes it went on over and over, and sometimes it was only once. It occurred in the sand, in the surf, and on the hard asphalt. It occurred with heavy boats on our heads – *that* was not fun, when we dropped, and the boat crashed down on top of us. We were being conditioned, like Pavlov's dogs, to react to the whistle. It would provide a safety control that was necessary when the explosions began.

The weekend before Hell Week we had both days to rest. My boat crew looked for any advantage we could think of. One crew member knew a nutrition expert who looked at the schedule and formulated three packages per day of vitamins, protein tablets, and salt pills to help us. The mix was based on what the nutrition expert thought we would need each day based on the schedule we knew about. We stocked these in our lockers to gobble down when events permitted. Future events would not allow us to follow that plan at all.

We also found a second inflatable floor board and stuffed it into our almost 300-pound black rubber Zodiac IBS to make it float higher in the water. The inflatable boat would be our constant companion – on our heads when walking – and our mode of transportation for the hours and hours of ocean paddling ahead. The bottom was a tough flexible rubber, and it had a two-inch-thick, inflatable floor that could be removed. The floor, when inflated properly, added strength, lift, and stability to the balloon-like craft. By putting two floor boards in the bottom, we added a few pounds of rubber weight, but we also added lots of air lift capability. We figured that this would help us ride higher in the water, and create less resistance as we paddled.

It also had a float tube that wrapped around the upper edge of the main boat tube, which was painted bright yellow for visibility purposes. This smaller outside tube made a good soft place to position a bent knee when paddling. We made sure this was pumped up hard so we could use it as intended.

"It pays to be a winner," was a quote we heard often, and knew it was true. Everything in First Phase seemed to be preparing us all for one event. It was.

Rumors said one winning boat crew would be secured early from the coming week. We all wanted to be in *that* crew. Every hour shaved off the planned endurance contest made finishing more possible. We purchased silicone spray and coated the entire outside of our boat with it, hoping to reduce bottom friction in the ocean races ahead.

We had all heard the story of another crew that had a better idea. Late on the night before Hell Week, their crew had taken a large tank of helium gas and filled the entire deflated boat with helium. An IBS back then was twelve feet long, six feet wide, and normally weighed over 280 pounds. They are lighter and smaller today. After filling it like a helium balloon, it would have almost no weight at all. This seemed like a brilliant maneuver to save the necks and backs of the entire crew. Unfortunately, they filled it in the cool evening air.

Breakfast, following their first disorienting night, came after only seven hours. The boat crew with the helium-filled boat was enjoying a much lighter than expected boat, and they were easily leading the runs. As always, each boat crew dropped their boat outside the mess hall and stationed one crew-member to guard the boat while others ate. He would be relieved by another crewman once feeding was maximized, and he would then run in to gorge on the hot mess hall offerings.

The sun was up when the boats were lined up side by side, and the entrance faced south. This was the warmest side of the building. Unfortunately, when helium warms, like all gasses, it expands. This makes the helium more buoyant.

As their class began to file out for the next event, the warm sun was causing one boat guard to sweat more than the others. His boat was floating three inches off the ground. He was trying to hold it flat with his boot on the bow, but that made the back end rise even higher. He could not sit on it, because he was on guard, and needed to be in a parade rest position, like the others.

It took the confused – and amused – first instructor out the door to notice this abnormality. It never occurred to him that a boat could be lighter than air, so he wandered over to look. Something was not right.

The boat crew saw the trouble coming, and ran over to take positions and hold the boat down. They were about to be discovered, and they knew it. One slight weather miscalculation was about to cost them dearly. And it did. They carried the boat back with an instructor standing inside the boat while rocking it back and forth. Refilled with air, it was then loaded with sand, and the day marched on.

Oops.

The boat crew is the component element for organization and accountability. As men quit, the seven-man boat crew would get smaller, but the boat would not get lighter. Once a boat crew was down to four or five men, the crews would be combined. If enough officers were left, each boat crew was allotted one officer. Leadership was always monitored in both officer and enlisted alike.

"Line up by height," called out an instructor, following a briefing about the upcoming Hell Week.

Lunch was over, and we still had the weekly timed four-mile run ahead. This was a new concept. Until now, height and weight and ability had not mattered. Now, it seemed the instructors were going to match heights to ensure each crew shared the same load on their heads when carrying their boat. This way, a short sailor would not be denied the opportunity to hold up his end of the boat.

"Time to pick boat crews. Do it now and do it fast," he repeated as we scrambled to follow instructions.

We all knew that there were seven men in a crew. Quickly, I realized that the first largest seven men would have a physical presence that might be advantageous in the competition ahead. Certainly, they might have some increased combined strength for events to come, and without a doubt, if I was an inch shorter than the others, the boat would feel somewhat lighter in the days ahead. A quick calculation indicated I might be the eighth or ninth tallest in our protracted line scrambling for position. I made a calculated move into the front part of the line, and made sure not to make eye contact with the instructors.

"One, two, three, four, five, six," I quickly counted, as I slithered quietly into the seventh place in line.

MM3 Dave Banton was sixth in line at five feet ten inches, and he glanced briefly at me as I sidled up next to him. I stood on my tip toes, and held fast as the rest of the class formed a snaking line.

"OK, count off one to seven," directed the instructor as we scrambled into line.

We did, and with each number "seven" we were pushed away with commands as "Boat Crew One, Boat Crew Two…" I called out "seven" and was now in boat crew one, where I wanted to be. Every little bit helped, I hoped.

"Now go get your boats ready."

I was sure some of others in the class saw what I had done, and I thought I saw a few interested glances, but it happened so quickly that I was allowed to get away with this bit of chicanery. I was now part of the biggest and tallest boat crew. To this day, I wonder if the instructors saw it, and if they did, perhaps they appreciated the move. After all, we were training to join a group where rules were simply *guidelines*. The other possibility was that they saw it, and they wanted to see how the rest of the boat crew or class handled my maneuver. Leadership works both ways.

Boat Crew One was now set, and the big boys had me as their officer to start. That was just stellar for me since I was still hiding behind one other officer in rank, and these men would give our crew a good chance to win in the upcoming competitive events. More importantly to me, I was hoping to save my neck, spine, and muscles by relying some on the bigger men in front supporting slightly more weight of the boat on their heads.

That Friday ended a bit early. It was 0200, and Instructor Steve Frisk was holding the stopwatch as the last of the runners passed him. This was the traditional Friday four-mile timed run, and once again every runner had made it in under the required thirty-two minutes. Winget and Johnson were first again. Rosensweig was last but smiling, as he slid past Frisk with twelve seconds to spare.

"Mr. Turk, gather your class over here," he directed, as Rosy bent over nearby to catch his breath.

The class assembled over in a festive mood. There would be no monster mash today for failed runners. Our Proctor Chief Puckett and Instructor Frisk waited as the gang organized into a tight knot.

"Gents, we are going to secure you early today and send you off to rest and eat and prepare for the week ahead. Chief Puckett and I are pleased with the forty-five of you that have made it this far. If you have not had a friend or a family member tell you that you are crazy to want to be a SEAL, then we are surprised. Next week will test you beyond even their imaginations, but you are all ready now. We have made you ready. The impossible awaits you."

Puckett and Frisk paused and looked around. They saw their own past teammates, and current friends' faces, in the gaggle around them.

"Those of you that complete next week, and *every one of you* are now capable of doing so, will take the first big step in joining a fraternity of men that have discovered that anything is possible.

"Starting Sunday night, you will be asked to endure what your family and friends will never understand. Your attempts to explain the significance of what you will accomplish will fall on deaf ears. They most likely believe it is impossible. You will learn that it is not."

Both instructors were smiling encouragingly as Frisk continued.

"Six days of impossible are waiting for you. You are ready. We believe in you, but only some of you know if you can do it. After much research, we still haven't figured out how to tell what it is that will allow you to succeed. So tonight, go eat, and rest, and be back on Sunday as briefed," he said. "The impossible awaits."

After a final formation, we were directed into the classroom and briefed about the plan for the upcoming week. We were reminded again to be back early on Sunday to await the midnight raucous start to the week we had been training for. There was a general feeling of dread mixed with excitement. We had learned all we could from Mike Suter, Frank Winget, and others who would share what they knew about the coming six days of Hell. We had hugged, and bragged, and promised, and spit, and done as many manly things as we could, to ensure each other that we would be there for mutual support in the week to come. And then, we went our separate ways.

The mood that weekend was entirely anticipatory. We all knew that the test we had been preparing for would start soon. We needed to eat and sleep and believe. The odds were against each of us, but we were in great shape now. Body fat was mostly gone, and muscles were strong, firm, and able to endure. I had gained ten pounds, and lost the baby fat from my shipboard time. MM3 Banton had gained thirty pounds of muscle. Sayre and McNabb weighed the same, for they had *come* with lots of muscle and no fat. McNabb was so lean, he sank in the pool while practicing drown proofing. Running, swimming, and paddling were second nature and did not require thought… just *endurance*.

Most were excited that the week we had been training for was at hand. Almost everyone used the next forty hours to be with family or friends, eat a lot, run a little, and rest.

On that Friday evening, I rode my Yamaha 250 street bike ninety minutes away to my sister's house near the beaches south of Los Angeles. I would eat and rest and worry with a focus on rest. I ran on the sandy beaches at a comfortable pace. Running was still not fun, but it was necessary.

On Sunday morning, it was time to return, so I began a leisurely ride back. The fun would begin this evening around midnight. I was thinking about the weather report. Every station was saying the same thing. We were facing a horrible week of rain and astringent cold every single day. Fishing boats were making different plans for the week ahead due to small craft warnings.

At 1100 that morning, I passed a familiar sign. It was twenty-four inches by thirty, and it had a white shield with a red cross through it. The left upper space of the shield was sky blue with an X formed by touching white stars. It was just like the sign my own Episcopal church posted, for all to see, as an invitation. I remembered that, most likely, service would just now be starting.

I turned left and followed the road to a church parking lot. I was wearing blue jeans, wind breaker, and a T-shirt and carried my helmet – I reminded myself that God did not care much about the clothes we wear. I walked in and took a seat in the last row. Incense lingered where the priestly procession had passed, and I knelt on the kneeling pad pulled down from the pew in front of me.

I wanted to ask God for a very special favor, but I was not an experienced man with prayer. The prayers I had learned by rote had no relevance, and the prayers I had prayed when younger were usually asking God to help me cope with life with an alcoholic father. I knew there was a God, however up close and very personal, and I knew he cared. I let the service happen around me as I prayed a simple prayer for sunshine.

Please Lord, do not let this coming weather happen to our class.

The winter Pacific water was so icy and penetrating it burned our skin this time of the year. If we had to deal with that, and the rain, *and* the wind, our chances would be poor at best. I noticed sympathy in the eyes of others as I made my way, under-dressed, to take communion that day. They could all tell that I was there for a reason, and I think their prayers followed me down the aisle.

To this day, I consider that the coming answer to my prayer was clearly a miracle. The thick dark clouds gathered over Coronado as I drove on and parked my bike in the garage. I packed and ate and dressed for the inevitable to begin that evening. I hitched a ride with a classmate to the barracks where we would rest and nap and worry about what was to come. Somewhere around midnight, it began, *just* as expected, and the sky was totally black with no stars visible in the night sky and a harsh, cutting wind.

The sun rose as scheduled the next morning to find us shivering, wet, and miserable, but not one serious drop of rain fell on our class all week long.

Miracles happen.

"That which does not kill us make us stronger."
—Friedrich Nietzsche

Chapter 7
It Begins Day 1

HOURS WITHOUT SLEEP - 0
CLASS MEMBERS - 7 OFFICERS AND 38 MEN
(INJURIES, VOLUNTARY DROPS, FAILED RUN/
SWIM STANDARDS HAVE COST THE CLASS 25
MEN ALREADY)

It began exactly when it was rumored to. Our lives exploded with blinding flash-bang grenades, screaming instructors, and the deafening sounds of automatic weapons of various calibers, firing on full automatic. Hot brass splattered and sprang and splashed into the puddles of wetness caused by roaring fire hoses accumulating on the asphalt outside the barracks. We had been laying quietly on well-made beds, fully clothed, but wide awake, waiting for the inevitable chaos that was scheduled to begin our torture. We had eaten our fill, and slept when we could, but we would find out, as all previous classed had, that no amount of preparation would ready us for these first few minutes.

I was sure that they would not kill us. They would scare us and test us at least as well as others had done before, but this marked the beginning of a very long, grueling test of endurance, fortitude, and learning about ourselves – one that most of us were looking forward to in a difficult-to-explain sort of way. Most of us were also waiting to find out if we would discover our physical and mental limits. If we found that legendary place where only the mind would control our destiny, then we would be given the opportunity to examine it, embrace the pain, and move far, far beyond it. Just knowing that this moment was coming – for those that would allow it to happen – was frightening enough for some to drop their helmets under the brass bell and walk away in just these first few minutes.

"Get yourselves back to your rooms and change into jocks and socks and come back carrying swim fins. You have one minute!" screamed an instructor.

I looked through the sprays from the multiple fire hoses being used to soak all of us and saw ENS John Muggs smile at me; we both twirled to follow this bizarre order. We had both seen and done this exercise in silliness multiple times at the US Naval Academy, and we knew what to do. In our rooms, we explained to the very confused to strip off their clothes and put on their jock straps while leaving their white socks on. Then grab the duck feet swim fins we were issued and run back down the stairs to stand inspection wearing only this bare version of clothing with helmets on heads and fins in our hands. ENS Muggs and I were already dressed as ordered and taking a few extra calming breaths while we waited for a few more to join us in this ridiculous attire. The guns were still making it difficult to hear, and the water was everywhere outside as instructors ran up and down the halls making new and different demands on those they found not ready.

"Where is your swim buddy? Do not lose your swim buddy. Get dressed and get down there now," directed an instructor while he tossed a flash bang grenade down the hall.

Flashes and ear-splitting explosions echoed off the walls as spent brass casings rolled at our feet.

"Jesus Christ, sir, what are we supposed to do?" quipped Rosensweig.

"Just make the uniform change, and get your ass back out there," said ENS Muggs. "This is all a game. Enjoy it."

He had seen all this before, and if this was the best they had to offer, this was going to be a breeze, he thought.

Confusion was rampant, disorienting, and intended. But this was just the beginning of a long, exhausting series of unexpected tasks designed to put the fear of God into us. Some have said it is like combat, where the unexpected is common, and the noise indescribable. It was designed to simulate just that. They were looking for warriors.

The early morning hours continued in chaos. Fire hoses sprayed chilly water and knocked trainees down. Flash bang grenades roared, and automatic weapons flashed all around. Brass shells covered the floor and made running more difficult. Group commands were mixed with individual orders to the trainees that appeared disoriented or confused. Confusion reigned. One man walked to the bell hanging close by, rang it three times, and walked defiantly away. No one heard it amongst the noise and thunder surrounding us, but it was expected to happen more than once. As soon as the bell rang, an instructor took the man by the arm and led him quickly away. No comment. No disparagement. He had made his choice, and now his life would take a different direction. He would be gone in a matter of minutes, and not seen again. Unless the quitter was your swim buddy or new close friend, there was not any time to consider what had happened or wonder why. The survival mode was in full swing, most were prepared for the noise and confusion, but a rare few were not. For some, there had never been a similar event in their lives that allowed them to experience personal chaos where they had no control. These were the ones that would quit in these first few minutes.

We were ordered back into our standard issue green pants, T-shirts, and boots. We were to have helmet liners tightly secured on our heads and kapok life jackets firmly tied on, as we marched into the raging Pacific Ocean to join arms and sing songs that we had been rehearsing all month. It was bleak, bitterly freezing water, and it pounded our backs with salty seaweed infused, pile-driver waves. Our feet and legs were going numb, and did not work well, when we were ordered to re-form in boat crews and begin the obstacle course. But now, in the near *total* darkness, we were directed to put our helmet liners in front of our faces and begin the course by feel only. We were stumbling forward together with officers and others trying to make order out of the impossible. Getting hurt was a fear we all felt. We had come a long way already, and a broken leg or sprained ankle could end it all.

The chaos finally slowed, and the lights in the nearby apartments flicked off as the curious occupants went back to bed. The phones stopped ringing at the police department, as confused area inhabitants figured out that the US soil was not being invaded by a hostile force. The police, of course, were *always* made aware of the coming start of Hell Week so they could reassure the populace, once again, that World War Three had not started in Coronado.

We were back under our boats, in our assigned crews, and only short one man in boat crew five. Kapok life jackets provided some padding and sense of warmth, but we were already shivering from the cold and adrenalin. Wide eyes were everywhere as the confusion settled down and order returned.

"Forward, double-time, march," came the command. "Mr. Turk, lead your men to the obstacle course. Bow touching stern, Gentlemen. Move out briskly."

And off we moved together towards the nearby obstacles. We passed the looming fifty-foot diving tower that would be part of our future dive training and listened to the surf pounding nearby.

"Fuck you, Chief Gosser," came a muffled yell from the darkness of the obstacle course, and we all froze in shock briefly, while moving blindly on, wondering which suicidal trainee had just condemned us all to a fate worse than death.

"*Who* said that?" came an outraged instructor's scream. "I will find out who you are, and when I get my hands on you I am going to bite your head off and use it to polish my boots."

Some sincerely believed this impossible threat and were looking for somewhere to hide. There was no place to go except *forward*; I stumbled into a stomach-high log obstacle that I knew I was supposed to climb over. I rolled over it, blindly knowing my face was now covered by the helmet liner, and I lay motionless in the sandy depression I slid into. I could hear furious instructors moving from student to student demanding satisfaction and promising mayhem to the offender that dared utter that foul threat.

"No sir! No Sir! No sir!" was repeated over and over, as they worked their way to my prostrate form.

I wondered how in hell we were going to get out of this mess, and who in the world thought they could get away with it. Could it be Mike who was in this third try at BUD/S and his second Hell Week? Was our senior NCO crazy enough, or brave enough, to do this? Did he think this might add some levity to the event? Perhaps it was one of the younger kids that had chosen this way to quit en route to ringing the bell. I was in a small panic as

I heard boots shuffle towards my shadowy, cowering, prostrate figure. There was another person lying flat, and breathing hard, near me.

"Get up you lazy bastards, we see you there. Did you insult Chief Gosser? Did you dare to challenge the manhood of a man who survived the jungles of Vietnam and led his team into to spit in the face of death? Did you?!"

"No sir," was all the man next to me could make himself mutter.

"Who was it, you slimy excuse for a tadpole? I am going to kill him myself, personally."

"I did not recognize the voice, Instructor. I am sorry," he stammered in fear.

"Well get your ass over the next obstacle and quit looking at me, you lazy piece of horse dung. If you want to lie down now, there is not much hope for you making it through the night because the rain is coming, and the pain is only just beginning. Plus, very soon, we are going to kill one of you, and roast him for a midnight snack."

I moved away also and quickly slammed into John, my compadre from the Academy.

"Holy crap, Muggs, did you say that? Do you know who did?"

"No way did I do it. I think it might have been another instructor."

And suddenly, it made more sense. We were not going to survive as individuals, and as a team, no one would have tried such a stunt. And damn, it had just the effect the instructors had wanted. It kept the panic and disorientation going. This was going to be a very long first night of a very long raw, wet, and sleepless week. There was not time to think about it. There was only time to keep moving. We all knew that, to succeed, we needed to finish one task at a time; one event at a time. This first dark morning was still very young.

It was supposed to rain all week, but God so far had intervened to give His blessing to this day, for no rain yet fouled the harsh and biting winter night air. The sand was soft like crushed ice, and frustrating. Running and walking on it was like moving in slow motion. It fought you each step. The ever-present crunchy soft green ice plant covered the dunes in patches like celery laid flat, but eating it was not very rewarding. Many of the class had tried it just to see if it was palatable. It was not, but it was soothing to lie on, and if you were careful, you could run on it, and lessen the sandy suck to your boots. Each of us, in our own time and way, had paused in the days before the start and prayed for help. We were a winter class, and winter classes had the lower graduation rates. Winter was bad enough, but freezing rain and the lack of sun to give momentary daytime respite was damnable.

The next thirty minutes found us climbing over wooden poles and over reverse-inclined walls with our almost 300-pound rubber boat burdens. One boat crew had an instructor standing in their boat, holding on to the bowline as he rode his boat like a surfer. He rocked back and forth and dared the crew to drop him. Helmets rubbed hair from shaved heads, and shoulders and necks screamed and strained with the additional weight. The pain initially was both surprising and barely tolerable, but as the hours wore on, the body and mind fought each other until the pain became part of the reality we were fighting to survive. Interestingly, over time pain becomes more tolerable because it is unavoidable.

There have been plenty of opportunities through the years to observe how pain can be pushed away. The POWs in Vietnam were hung by their arms tied behind their backs until joints dislocated and skin turned blue from lack of circulation. Often it was the cessation of constant pain that became the most intolerable. When circulation returned to numb extremities, the pain flooded back with unimaginable electric heat. The same was true of the weight of the boats filled with sand or water – or an instructor – as it pushed down on neck bones and shoulder muscles. Logs held over the heads until circulation failed created a need to ignore it or collapse. In many cases, a punishment consisting of a return to frigid Pacific waters would blissfully rescue injured tissue and chemically begin to repair torn muscle fibers.

The blind obstacle course event this night had lasted an hour, and resulted in scrapes and bruises and more confusion.

"Down boats. Line up your boat crews for a safety brief," roared the bullhorn at the end of the chaotic event.

We all lined up alongside our boats in a close gaggle of boats and men. The instructor began to outline our next event. We would be going to do the feared rock portage event by paddling our boats to the rock jetty in front of the Hotel del Coronado. We would then bring in our boats, one at a time, aiming for a light held by an instructor. This was the event we had practiced in the daytime, but had never done at night. It was frightening in the daytime, as the coxswain ordered the boat crew to "paddle" or "hold water" while he tried to time the waves so that the boat could glide in on a swell, and not crash hard on the huge boulders ahead. It was going to be horrific in the pitch black of night.

"Gentlemen, this is a dangerous event, as you know. You have practiced it enough, but the waves are high tonight, and the bay is very dark. Keep your lifejacket straps tight. Work together, get out of the boat quickly, and over the slippery rocks before the next wave crashes your boat into you. Don't lose your paddles, and don't lose your boat. This is a graded exercise, and winners have more fun.

"The ocean swells tonight are four to five feet with an interval of twenty seconds. Watch out for your swim buddy, Gents. We have a long way to go tonight, and you don't need to start it injured."

"Well, here we go," whispered Randy as he lined his boat crew up for one more trip into Neptune's lair.

Rosensweig sidled up to him and sighed. "Keep us going straight please."

"Up boats, low carry," commanded Randy. "Let's get this done." And with a collective groan, his crew marched forward into the foamy sea of waves and wind.

"Fuck me," moaned Rosy as his boots filled with seawater, and he moved deeper into the night sea. He was more than waist-deep when the order came.

"Ones in."

He and his swim buddy tucked their paddles under the rubber cross tubes and dragged themselves into position, pulled out their paddles, and reached out together, to pull the boat forward with coordinated paddle pulls.

"Twos in; threes in," added Randy as he pulled his muscular body up quickly into the aft area of the boat. He stuck his paddle into the water behind him.

"Pull together," he ordered in a firm voice as the first of many waves tried to push them back to shore. It worked. They were outside the surf zone and somewhat alone in the dark cloud-covered night ocean. This was a brief respite that they were all enjoying as the other boats began their own battles with the surf and wind.

One by one, each boat crew entered the rolling surf zone. One by one, we paddled past the breaking surf, performed the required dump boat procedure where we pulled the boat upside down. All paddlers entered the numbing Pacific and then righted the boat by pulling it back over with ropes and handles. One crew had miss-timed the waves and had washed ignominiously back to shore. They were met by disgruntled instructors, ordered to recover lost paddles, subjected to push-ups in the surf while trying to control their boat, and had to re-launch to threats of greater punishments if failure followed again. They made it out the second time and joined the happily resting line of boats, making their way slowly north toward the rock jetty. The last boat paddled faster to catch up, but they, like the rest, were enjoying the sudden dark instructorless silence as they moved closer to the daunting task one mile ahead.

There was some light chatter of fear or encouragement as focus turned to the scary rocks ahead in the distance. The ambulance moved slowly along the beach – the line of boats visible by night vision scope – and monitored their progress.

ENS Randy Albracht was the coxswain in his IBS, and he lined up his boat to make the first run in. Six other men stood poised to paddle as he timed the swells. He was watching the light on the rocks, held by a watchful Instructor Steve Frisk, when he judged the time right he gave the "ready to begin" signal.

Randy had a wife and two young boys at home who had followed him first to Pensacola, Florida, for flight school, and they were now here in Coronado. He had left the boonies of Iowa on a quest for adventure and fame. Two children and a beautiful wife had checked the adventure box in his mind, but he was still looking for the fame.

Since he had been a champion collegiate wrestler and in the best shape of his life, he had chosen SEALs for the fame part, once being a pilot was not made available at flight school last year.

He had no idea how to swim with fins on, but no one had mentioned that requirement. He did have a triangular upper body with very little fat, and after some time at the Pensacola beaches, he looked like a frogman. He was sure it would offer more opportunity than his Iowa State history degree did.

He had never swum with fins before training but thought, *Hey, they most likely teach that, right?* So off he went, with wife and children in tow. Now he was faced with the reality of his choice.

"All paddle," he ordered, and the boat surged forward with a swell. They could ride the wave for a few seconds, and then the swell moved on without them. The light on the rocks was closer and illuminating the white spray of the waves that slithered and crashed ahead. The rocks were not actually visible yet.

"Hold water," he ordered, and all six paddles bit into the sea. He was unsure, but he did not allow his voice to show it. He took a deep breath and let the waves talk to him. Twenty seconds between swells and the rocks seemed close enough to make the final run in.

"All paddle," he cried with confidence, and the boat moved with intent. The men worked together as practiced, and the huge rocks suddenly appeared through the dark. Glistening and slippery, they reached out maliciously toward the inflatable, fourteen-legged-balloon heading their way.

"Ones out," he commanded quickly as the boat slammed into the first craggy, slimy boulder. On order, the first two men in the front jumped out with the forward boat lanyard in hand. They pulled tight to hold the boat against the rocks.

"Twos out. Threes out," he continued, while he prepared to scramble forward to the bow. This ordered the remaining four paddlers out of the boat. This all needed to happen in about three seconds before the next wave hit. They almost made it.

As his heavy framed body made it to the bow, a wave came. The back of the boat rose with the swell, and he fell forward onto the rocks head first. His helmet met the rocks, and the boat slipped sideways on top of him. The men holding the bowline held tight and could no longer see their officer. They were more focused on the number two man now trapped between the boat gunnels and the rock. It was Greg, a small man with great stamina. His large kapok lifejacket engulfed him. He was stuck there, and scrambling with hands and boots to get away. The boat floated away as the white foam exploded all around him, and he stepped free onto the first large rock.

For the moment, he was free, he paused a bit too long to ponder, and much to his surprise, he still held the wooden paddle in his left hand. He stepped gratefully forward to the next rock as the next wave crashed into him. This allowed the bowline men to pull the boat forward onto the rocks. Two things then happened simultaneously. ENS Albracht surfaced with wide eyes and a deep exhalation and took a lifesaving breath. Simultaneously, Greg was pushed forward toward shore where he felt his boot slide down the rock, as he buckled into a fetal position to brace for impact on the rocks below him. His right knee hit first, and took the entire weight of his body and wet kapok lifejacket full force on one knee. The pain was like what he imagined a lightning strike would feel like. He crumpled forward into the ocean and let the Pacific's icy fingers ease his pain somewhat. He was floating, his paddle was gone, and he lost focus on the task at hand. Only he knew what had happened. Everyone else was conducting their own personal survival exercise as choreographed in past events. Do your job, and count on the others to do theirs.

An instructor, and a boat crew member, fished Greg out of the froth, as he washed up on shore, with the pain in his knee partially numbed by the icy water. A corpsman was called over as the pissed-off instructor stopped yelling, suddenly noting the pain on Greg's face. This was trouble. Greg knew he was hurt, but this was the first major event, and dammed if he was going to stop now. He stood in pain as the corpsman examined him and winced deeply when his right knee was touched.

"Are you OK?" asked the corpsman.

"I am fine," he replied as he leaned on his boat crew partner, who had just found him. Swim pairs were required to stay together always.

"I think we should take you in for a better look," the corpsman replied in doubt. But his boat crew was all ashore now, and ENS Albracht had gathered his team and boat together.

"We will take care of him," the officer stated firmly, but he was unaware of the severity of Greg's pain, as two other men put Greg's arms around their shoulder and marched him onward to their next objective. They were all aware that they were being watched, and they needed Greg, and knew Greg needed them.

They had to cross the entire beach and carry the boat to the next event, over a half mile away – across Coronado Boulevard and onto the Naval Amphibious base. They did not know that the next event would test them all to the limit of their cold-water endurance.

The enormous and frightening surf had crashed us all into the unforgiving rocks and many were bleeding at knees and elbows while we helped carry our rubber boats to the Glorietta Bay area across the beach and then across the four-lane road to the Naval Amphibious Base waters. Two more men had asked to quit, from two different crews, and we were only hours into the first night. So, two more boat crews were down to six men each. This made it harder on those crews, and they were more angry than surprised at the deserters.

After a formal muster at the steel dock pointing out into the bay, we were all ordered to drop boats and tread water in the frigid bay while simultaneously stripping naked with boots tied around our necks and soggy socks stuffed inside. This was the drown-proofing exercise we had been taught in the nice warm pool weeks before. We had to tread water in the frigid evening bay as we undressed to make floats from our shirts and pants. There was still most of the original group left, and the water was white with froth as everyone slammed the water with cupped hands and tried to stay afloat by pushing air into our clothing floats.

The dark water was sucking the heat out of our muscles, and Greg was now having a grim time floating. His knee pain was seemingly better, bathed in the numbing waters. His swim buddy watched him closely, as he seemed almost asleep at times. Suddenly, Greg's eyes closed, and he sank unresponsive off his inflated pants float and down toward the dark water below. It was only ten to fifteen feet deep pier-side, where the chaotic treading of water was continuing, but suddenly Greg was gone. Rosy, his assigned swim buddy, waited a few seconds to register what had happened and then realized Greg was in trouble, and no one knew.

ENS Randy Albract was nearby and saw Greg's arm go under. He moved over quickly and grabbed for the disappearing arm.

Rosy and Randy were naked except for the socks and pair of boots tied around their necks. Rosy dove underwater and frog-kicked to his swim buddy's body moving slowly downward. Randy grabbed his arm and pulled him back to the surface while Rosy pulled upward.

"Corpsman! Help! Man down!" Randy yelled. He did not know what to do. They were close to the pier where Instructor Thornton could relay a yell for the corpsmen. They swam through the froth with few even noticing what was going on. They had Greg in a rescue hold now, and were moving to the nearby ramp where two corpsmen were wading in quickly to them.

We were down another classmate, and only the instructors knew how many of our class remained.

Greg was gone. He had begun breathing on his own as soon as he was brought to the surface, but he was rushed to the hospital by ambulance where they discovered that his right knee cap was shattered into three pieces. No one could understand how he had endured the half mile march with boat on his head to begin this last evolution in Glorietta Bay. This was not the first time the doctors and corpsmen at the base had seen men come to them after doing what seemed impossible. They all had stories to tell of Hell Weeks past, and it usually earned them a beer or two in telling it to an awed bar crowd.

ENS Turk, as class leader, was uncontrollably shivering, but physically unscathed by the rock portage event. His boat crew had done everything exactly as planned. He was, however, quite shaken by the event. He had been sure he would die, but the training had kicked in. He gave the right orders, at the right time, and they completed the event. His heart had never slowed down, and now he was colder than he had ever been in his life and keeping himself afloat in dark, bottomless water again. He paddled himself quietly to the pier and held on to one of the pilings while his swim-buddy treaded water nearby. He was seen by an instructor, however, and ordered away from the pier. There was splashing and confusion and yelling over loudspeakers. It was disconcerting and *almost* overwhelming after being smashed by Pacific Ocean waves onto the rocks only minutes before. He was whispering to his buddy to stay close and keep quiet as he wrapped his arms around the pier piling again. This deep, dark, frigid water was never part of his prior Army training, and no one had told him to expect it.

"Mr. Turk," screamed the bullhorn, "if you do not let go of the piling we will assume you have quit."

He did not let go. He couldn't. And just as suddenly as Greg, he too was gone. There were now only six officers left. Unbeknownst to most, except their own boat crew, one sailor had also quit after rock portage.

ENS Turk, ex-Army green beret, would return a year later to try again with a later class, but he would not make it that time either. ENS Holloway had broken his leg earlier and was waiting for another class, so both of our more senior officers were gone.

The bullhorn blared again.

"Mr. Adams, are you down there, or have you drowned yet?"

I answered carefully, in a tentative voice, from the dark water below, that I was still alive.

"Congratulations sir, you are the new class leader. Mr. Turk just quit."

"Oh shit," I mumbled out loud, but it was drowned out by all the others echoing the same sentiment even louder. It would be impossible to hide now. I was in trouble again, only five hours into the week. My plan to remain invisible was now history.

Greg had almost drowned, and ENS Turk and Greg, had suddenly disappeared. Rosy and Turk's swim partners now connected and were swim buddies surviving together.

At that time no one in training history had ever died in Hell Week.

That fact would sadly change one day.

Our class leader was now gone like a ghost in the night. Once the decision was made, exit from training was as fast and private as possible. Ridicule was not allowed or encouraged. Promises of hot soup and warm blankets were immediately acted on. But the trainee that had reached his limit was gone in an instant. The Navy community wanted and *needed* good men, but there was no place in the Teams – this day or any day in the future – for a quitter. They needed *someone special*, and they were clear about exactly what that meant.

The biting cold was everywhere. We were naked except for boots and socks hanging around our necks, as underwear was still forbidden. We were floating on the air-filled pants or uniform shirts that we had filled by splashing air into them. It was not difficult, as we had been trained to make survival bladders from our clothing. You tie the arms and legs with a knot at the end, and you button the buttons. Then it is a simple matter of splashing water and air into the remaining opening. The effort, in the astringent and exacting water, was exhausting especially when you also had to keep an eye on your swim buddy at the same time. God forbid, you lose sight of him. But once the clothing becomes your life raft, it is just a matter of making enough movement to avoid catching an instructor's eye. Now is not the time to be a winner. Now is the time to hide in the darkness of the surrounding waters. Conserve energy, and avoid burning more calories that will be needed more and more as we wait for sunrise.

Forty-five minutes passed slowly, and shivering increased again in earnest. Each man was alone with his thoughts. It was early still, and much was ahead. Personally, I again reminded myself that all the men around me were doing what needed to be done, and if they could do it, I sure could do it too.

"How's the water temperature, Gents?" asked the bullhorn.

"Warm and toasty, Instructor," came the pre-programmed response. There was little enthusiasm in the response, and the chattering-teeth sounds seemed louder. Instructors monitored the time in the water, calculated the effect of water temperature, and decided to end the exercise before hypothermia made it impossible to continue.

"Mr. Adams, get your class out of the water and form up for exercises," screamed the bullhorn.

We were down to thirty-nine now. There was a metal ladder that led to the dock floor. The floor was covered with standard amphibious metal tracks used to give traction on sand to vehicles off-loading from ships to the assaulted beaches. It did not seem possible, but the metal was even chillier than the water we had just scrambled out of.

We were down two officers and three other men, and the night was young.

"Give me a count," blurted the amplified voice.

"Sir, we are thirty-nine men now," I said, after each boat crew checked in. Over thirty helmets lined the distant rock hard sidewalk under the brass bell, all of them were stenciled with our class number.

One of those helmets might have belonged to ENS Holloway, but he had not quit, so it was not on display. After breaking his leg on the obstacle course, he was rolled back to the next class where he would complete his subsequent training with honors.

This was the reason I suddenly found myself in charge. Both men senior to me were gone. I was facing an additional challenge that I had not anticipated. As Chief Rogers reminded us all, "you will need to demonstrate that you can lead me into combat. Fail that test, and you are history."

"Holy Crap."

"Flutter kicks, Gentlemen. On your backs," came an order from amid the chaos.

We all throw down our wet uniforms and drop our almost-naked bodies flat onto the penetrating, unfriendly metal amphibious tracks we were standing on. Our boots were still hanging around our necks, where we placed them while treading water. It felt like our skin was sticking to the freezing metal. A few unthinking souls tried to get the boots off their necks to place by their pile of dripping uniforms. This made them appear slow to follow commands, and the instructors attacked. Push-ups, flutter kicks, and buckets of icy water were delivered with a vengeance. Confusion reigned.

Naked and wet in the darkness – with a cold breeze sucking the water off our skin – was as discomforting as is sounds. A wind on wet skin sucks all by itself, but as evaporation occurs, the cold gets colder. As liquid changes to a gas, physics teaches us that energy is required. That energy was quickly sucked from our bodies with a vengeance. There was no way to avoid it. Movement made it worse. We all found ourselves trying to hold still in hopes that the stinging metal under us would gain a few degrees, as we lay flat, and hid from the air moving around us. That saved a few heat calories as exercise kept the core temperatures safe.

Then came the hoses. Water sprayed like stinging rain from behind the spotlights. There was groaning. and cussing, and whispers of encouragement.

"Don't let this get to you." "Hang in there, buddy." "We can do this."

But like a deer in the headlights, I was now the new class leader amid the confusion. I would be ordered to do extra push-ups when anyone failed. But now, I was learning that I preferred the leaning rest position to lying flat on the wavy unforgiving chilled metal. I tried to cope with the extraordinarily unpleasant realization that I would not be able to hide anymore. Our ex–Green Beret class leader and Army Ranger officers were both gone. I would forever be the first in line or giving the marching orders as we moved from event to event.

This realization seriously sucked, as we were now only a few hours into what would feel like an interminable week of hell. The water spray hit me square in the face as I looked up to see a smiling instructor enjoying the chaos.

"No man ever achieved worthwhile success who did
not, at one time or other, find himself with at least one
foot hanging well over the brink of failure."
—Napoleon Hill

Chapter 8
First dawn Monday Day 1

HOURS WITHOUT SLEEP - 6
6 OFFICERS AND 33 ENLISTED

It was dark and breezy. We were dressed in our wet uniforms and wet sandy kapok lifejackets. There were six or seven men in each group, lined up again under their black rubber boats. It was time to move to the next evolution.

"Double-time, march," came the order, and our line of boats snaked along the blacktop road toward the BUD/S area where we would be directed to change into dry clothes and boots. Some socks and T-shirts had been lost at sea during the long drown-proofing event. We ran upstairs to our rooms, with threatening commands following us, to avoid being the last one back.

Some of us gobbled the vitamins we had stashed, and others stuffed Snickers bars in their mouths, and pockets. We all gathered quickly for muster at our boats after a very quick change of clothes – and the last man out was ordered to "hit the tub."

Next to the PT podium sat an old iron claw-foot bathtub filled with water. Our last man out was identified and directed to the tub. It was ENS Fields. He ran over, stepped in with his new dry boots, and slowly, painfully immersed himself in the icy water, lifejacket and all. He ran back to his boat for the one and a half mile run to the Amphibious Base pool, but his tentative self-dunking was determined to be too slow.

"*Everyone* hit the surf. Mr. Fields has forgotten about the mission. You will complete our orders briskly, and with enthusiasm, Gentlemen, or you will pay a price. Please make sure to thank your classmate for this moment. Now, hit the surf."

There were groans, and many hard looks were directed at our confused and embarrassed classmate, who thought he had done it fast enough. Paddles were quickly stowed, and the entire class moved together to the plunging waves behind us.

ENS Vernon Fields was a recent graduate of his state college. He was the pride of his family, as the first officer to serve his country. His father had just finished thirty years on ships and had retired as a Master Chief. He looked a bit gaunt for his chosen profession, but so did many of us. The muscles would be added to all of us soon enough. He was his family's first college graduate, but his family had many that had served in the military for generations. He had majored in English, and with his community college plus state college time, he had earned a two-year NROTC scholarship, a degree, and a commission in the Navy.

Becoming a SEAL was his own idea. He intended to make his father prouder than he already was. He had the motivation and had paid his own way through college by working menial labor jobs. He was certain he could complete the training. But in some ways, he stood out from the others. He was not a sports enthusiast, and he had not played any sports in high school or college. He was a loner, and he ran alone to get in shape. He did not enjoy running or swimming, but he could do both well. It would be his will to succeed that would get him through. Of that he was sure.

"Stay together," ENS Muggs encouraged. "No stragglers, or we might have to do this again." He was thinking ahead and nurturing our sense of teamwork. It would pay off. We all arrived back at the boats wet and together. The instructors circled us looking for weakness, but we appeared ready and unified, so the next evolution began.

As the line of black IBSs and gaggle of legs moved like a centipede towards the pool, we passed a huge double-barreled ship's gun – a memorial from

World War II. We had all passed it many times, and no one had a reason to read the brass plaque or learn its history. It was always there. Now we were focused on other things again, until....

"Listen up tadpoles! Who knows your naval history here?" yipped an instructor over the bullhorn.

"This gun monument we are passing is from World War II, and it is part of your heritage. It is a basic Mark 1, Mod 2, BFG. Now, who knows what BFG stands for?" he inquired quite seriously.

There was a pause as we all searched for the answer. Then from under one boat came the answer.

"Big Fucking Gun! Instructor."

That's right, God damn it! Brilliant job, Petty Officer Suter. You may fall out from under you boat now."

And as he did so, the instructor's whistle sounded one long shrill tweet. As trained, everyone dropped to the asphalt, and covered their heads, while the suddenly legless boats dropped down on top.

Two whistle blasts sounded, and with boats on top, everyone began a slow, scraping, low crawl towards the sound.

Mike Suter was confused. What was he supposed to do? His boat crew was gasping, and slithering along in front, as he stood there. The instructors seemed to have forgotten him... or *not*. So, he made the call himself, and dove under his boat back into the position where he had been, and slipped along with the rest. Team.

Three whistles signaled the recovery order, and all the boats rose together, reformed the snake-like line of rubber and legs, and began to move again.

The instructors *did* notice Mike's actions, and they nodded to each other. This was a man that just might have what they were looking for. Team.

As we neared the pool area, boats again on our heads, we could hear the saltwater of the bay squishing from our socks and out of our boots. Feet are essential to every event. We had been cautioned not to remove our boots. Inside each boot was a swollen foot. They would swell more if the boots were removed, and they would not easily get back into the boot. The skin was white and wrinkled, some toes were bleeding. Most feet were already blessedly numb, but many screamed in pain with each unwanted footfall.

Toenails were starting to loosen, and many would fall off later as *trench foot* settled in.

Trench foot, or immersion foot, was a well-known problem in Vietnam, and all our instructors and corpsmen were combat veterans from that war. Chronic exposure to wet leads the skin and nails to literally rot. Blood supply is cut off by swelling, and soft tissue begins to die, and blisters often form. Tiny vessels and nerves were sometimes damaged beyond repair. Those of us that dragged our damaged bodies to the end of Hell Week would discover, months later, that the body can usually repair the damage, but it would be a long hard-fought battle.

The sun was due to rise soon, but the wind was still severe. The sound of waves crashing on the distant beach was lost to ears focused only on hearing what needed to be heard. Focus must always be on the moment at hand. To think about tomorrow is to invite failure. There is no tomorrow. There is only now. Complete this task now, and just take one step at a time.

Interestingly, the bay and ocean water surrounding Coronado is never *ever* warm. The Alaskan current brings in the icy waters that flow from Alaska to Japan right back to Coronado, California, on its oval path, back to Alaska. Damn King Neptune.

It was now 0430 on a clear, forbidding, windy, dark morning, and the pool was lit darkly, so our soon-to-be-naked, shivering bodies would not be easily on display to the women's barracks nearby. Rumors were that they looked forward to these events, and often assembled at windows to watch. We gathered, as directed, at the shallow end of the pool. There were blue and gold lane dividers marking the lap lanes.

"It is relay race time, Gents. Take your uniforms off and line up your naked, ugly bodies by boat crew for towel relay races. Each swimmer will take one of these white towels into each hand, and when we start the race, you will jump in, do a forward flip, and then swim down and back with the towels in your hands. There are some hot showers in the locker room behind you," teased the instructor temptingly.

I counted out twenty quick push-ups as ordered for something someone else had done and stripped down along with everyone else, while the instructors harassed the others individually. So far, I felt lucky. The class was keeping together and following commands well, so I rushed into the crowd to hide.

The crowd pushed ENS Johnson forward to the starting slot for his boat crew. He was one of our best runners, but naked now. We were all naked, and the wind was blowing us closer together. Modesty was taking a back seat to survival. The wind would blow, and we would huddle closer. It was embarrassing to feel a naked man's ass push up against whatever body part it could find, but the instant warmth was a pleasant surprise, and we all mostly pretended not to notice as the circle of flesh condensed into a smaller mass to share needed warmth. Survival was already important, and we had a long way to go.

The pool water, however, was delightfully warmer. The wind was agonizingly unsympathetic.

"Go," came the start command, and ENS Johnson jumped into the pool with a towel in each hand. The first freestyle stroke was slow as the towel filled itself with pool water and tried to drag him with it. However, the pool water was relatively warm and he liked that. Stroke by heavy stroke, we watched as he fought across the pool and back. The race was on, and some faint cheering was heard at the shallow end. It was exhausting, and we were not sure how best to cover the distance. I tried side stroke, but that did not work any better, so we all splashed and crawled to the finish.

"Here," Johnson panted to the next swimmer, handing him the towels as he dragged his wet burdens up to the next swimmer, who gratefully leaped in and flipped over his head. ENS Johnson climbed out and immediately wanted back in the water. The wind was carving icy rivulets along his spine. The gaggle of gasping men was grinding closer, and shifting to stay on the leeward side.

ENS John Johnson was well prepared physically and was now looking back on his life to date. He had succeeded in everything he had ever attempted. School was never difficult, sports seemed to come naturally, and women would hang on his every word, even when there was no alcohol involved. He had been planning to join the Navy early in college, in part because he knew he would look great in uniform. When he wore the summer white uniform, he looked like a recruiting poster for the Navy – or for a local modeling agency. He had no scars. He had never been in a fist fight because he was smart enough to walk away. He exuded confidence and demonstrated ability in everything he did. His girlfriend was proud of him, and they talked often about how much fun they would have together in the future with his Navy officer's pay. She liked to go out to dinner, since her cooking skills lagged far behind her natural beauty.

The hard-hearted wind blowing that morning did not let up, and we remained roughly lined up, naked, with towels in each hand. The relay races continued, and feigned enthusiasm was squeaked loudly by the shivering crowd, to please the instructors. Each line of men was jumping and cheering for the swimmer in the pool as he tried to swim twenty-five meters down and twenty-five meters back with a towel in each hand. This activity was at least distracting, as we waited to get back into the warmer water. Once in the water, it was like swimming in syrup with weights pulling both arms backwards, and fatigue came quickly. The less experienced swimmers were having a very difficult time. The instructors made note.

"Nuts to butts," was the unspoken order of the day as we drew closer and touched. One touch at a time was met with one ignored glance at a time, and again the huddle collapsed upon itself as each new swimmer returned. The coldest were the recent relay swimmers, wet all over, as the wind would freeze dry them while trying successfully to lower their body temperatures. Just as a leeward place was found, it was time to jump into the pool and do it again. The noise from teeth chattering was quite distracting.

Seaman Apprentice McNabb was the junior ranking enlisted man. He had married the woman of his dreams just before coming here. He looked like a frogman from the movies. He was tanned, muscular, and might have been carved from stone by an ancient Greek sculptor. He knew demanding farm work, and it showed. Nothing ever seemed to upset him. He would laugh at most challenges with a confidence in himself that seemed inappropriate for his youthful age. He was a natural leader, and people just instantly liked him.

He was working his way into the middle of the pile of flesh that was his team and trying to ready himself for the task ahead. He swam well, but he was literally all muscle, and he sank easily. As he awaited his inevitable turn in the relay, he wondered how he would do with towels in each hand. He looked around him and saw the others. They were all mostly smaller than he was. He was wondering if he could keep up with them. He was stronger, and bigger, and tougher, and he knew it. The cold was sucking the life out of him, and the wind was stinging his skin. He wondered how these other men could handle what he could not. He was sure of one thing – if *they* could do it, *he* could do it. Then the call came to make his way down the lane with towel in each hand... naked... cold... and confused.

With a splash he was in the pool, and the water was warmer then air assaulting him seconds ago. He slowed down, and sank with each stroke. The instructors already knew he was a muscle-bound swimmer that sank. He was milking this for all it was worth. His frog kicking legs were doing much of the work now.

Thank you, warm water.

But then it ended, and the next swimmer was pulling him out by the towels in his hands. There were mock cheers going on around him, since everyone knew there would be no winner tonight. He leapt athletically from the pool smiling, and was again assaulted by the wind.

"McNabb, that was too slow. Your team is losing because of you," jeered an instructor. "Get over here and take these two fire buckets. Get in the pool and do it one more time."

Damn! Piss in my boots! he thought and then began to doubt himself.

Would they endure when he might not be able to? Were they stronger than him?

No, no one is stronger than me.

And then he listened to himself and looked at the pain and fear in the other faces around him slowly moving together for warmth.

If they can do it, I can do it.

He had *not* come here to fail. This was a challenge he expected. He liked the effort required, but it seriously sucked now. He grabbed the buckets, jumped in with a loud "Hooyah, Instructor," and almost walked across the pool bottom, pulling the buckets with him. He thought he was going to drown. The monitors watched his struggle carefully.

Not bad, they thought, as he improvised to survive.

"Seaman Sayre, you are part fish. I have never seen anyone swim with towels as fast as you just did. Your team wins the relay, so you may take them into the hot showers for five minutes while we help the rest of the class understand the concept of losing."

Sayre and his team of six naked, shivering warriors – including ENS Johnson – trotted to the pool showers nearby and cranked on the hot water. It felt good, and color returned to their fingers and toes. They just stood and waited, trying to absorb as much heat as possible. It *seemed* like a good reward.

It was not.

In walked the First Phase officer, LT Scotty Lyons, and everyone froze in place.

LT Lyons was wearing a long cowboy type outer oilskin garment with deep pockets. He broke a smile, and pulled out a bottle of peppermint schnapps.

"Pass this around, Gents. It might warm your innards," he commanded after taking a swig for himself.

It smelled good, and they passed it around quickly while staying in the nice warm water. Their fingers and toes tingled with renewed circulation. There was a slight and immediate buzz felt by all.

"ENS Johnson, get your boat crew out here and join your class," came the order one minute later. The class was starting to dress again back into the wet uniforms that lay in a line by their boots. The wind was sucking at their glowing red skins as they began to dress.

"Jesus Christ. These clothes are cold," whispered Sayre to ENS Johnson, his swim buddy, as he pulled up his soaking wet wind-refrigerated pants. The wind whipped away any warmth they had stored, and everything seemed much colder.

"Ya think?" muttered his buddy miserably.

The brief heat break had seemed heavenly, but now, as the body tried to conserve that heat once again, the stinging cold was attacking their collective minds and bodies all over again. They had to adjust back to the point of numbness. It was taking too long. The instructors circled and cajoled.

"Do you want to call it a night, Sayre? There is a hot chocolate, schnapps, and more hot showers waiting for you next to your soft comfortable bed. We have a very long way to go tonight and tomorrow and on, and on?"

"No thank you, Instructor. We are warm and toasty now," he crooned defiantly.

Seaman Apprentice Don Sayre had come from a dirty backward town in Peoria, Illinois. He had been adopted and thought of himself as a bastard raised by his much older chain-smoking parents. He learned to fight and learned about discrimination and hate in school. He got away from home by swimming and playing hockey for his high school. He was a superb athlete and swimmer and could have gone to college on a full scholarship, if he had wanted, but two houses away lived a man had who enthralled him with his endless stories of seemingly exciting and rewarding past times in the Navy UDT/SEAL teams. So here he was.

"On your feet," blared an instructor, after ordering the so-called *seven dwarfs* boat crew to hold in the leaning rest position, following twenty more push-ups, for coming in last. The dwarfs were the seven shortest men and constituted boat crew seven, but they showed the most guts, all the time.

They climbed painfully to their feet and stood at attention.

"Finish getting your clothes on, Gentlemen, we have places to go."

So, as quickly as their frozen fingers and toes would allow, they slipped and slithered into their wet, crusty, wind whipped uniforms. The stinging cloth grabbed at their partially numbed red skins and scraped at everyone like fingernails of ice. First, the socks and T-shirts, then the pants and shirts, and finally the boots were dragged on over soggy socks. We laced them up with no awareness of the swelling feet that would be worsening soon.

Our rubber boats awaited us outside the pool entrance in neat order. With helmets back on our heads, we were ordered to re-form underneath the boats. With boats touching front to back, we started a crazy mile-long jog to the obstacle course. As we approached the amphibious base stoplight that would direct us across the street, a shrill whistle blew. One whistle blast.

We all dropped hard to the pavement. The heavy rubber boats bounced off our backs. Two blasts, and we began to crawl toward the source. The gravel ground scraped our knees and elbows raw, but we made it to the instructor with the evil whistle. This would go on every day and night until we made it to our demolition "So Solly Day" on Thursday. These whistle commands would be part of the safety conditioning in place to ensure no one died when the coming beach explosions would test each of us in a loudly unique way. It was still Monday morning.

Three tweets on the whistle, and we were back on our feet, with boats on our heads, watching the stoplight turn green. There were no cars visible in either direction this early in the dark morning of our first day.

Boat crew two, led by ENS Muggs, trotted up to the stoplight next to our crew. He was tall, powerful, and quiet. He was standing and waiting patiently with his boat and crew, in a clump of ice plant, with his wet clothes covered in the fine sand it grows in. He had just finished push-ups for his boat crew's failure to keep up. He always did what was asked, and did not complain. He stood five feet ten inches tall with short cropped light brown hair. He would box the 185-pound class at the next amphibious base boxing intramural and would win in the first round without his opponent even touching him. He was a New York State Golden Gloves champion boxer and was quick and tough.

He graduated from the Naval Academy, and his higher class standing allowed him to obtain one of the rare slots, allowing him to come to BUD/S directly from the Academy. He knew how to perform under pressure. He just kept going, seemingly unfazed by the monumental tasks at hand. I was grateful to have him leading the boat crew next to me. As the current class leader, I could be – and often *was* – held accountable for anyone's failure.

Two more senior officers were gone already. John really wanted me to succeed as class leader. He knew it, and I knew it, but we did not speak of it. We were operating as a leadership team now and had promised each other that we would ensure completion together. Otherwise, the job would fall to him next. His thoughts were shrouded, as always, behind a hard visage of determination. We all thought he likes us, at times, and he did nothing to dispel those thoughts, but his thoughts were always his own, and we would never discover them clearly.

Draw no unwanted attention to yourself – it was a well understood tactic for survival.

It was still an hour until breakfast as we lined up as a class as usual for PT. We knew this routine well, and it was somewhat comforting to be back in a familiar place doing familiar things. Flutter kicks, sit-ups, push-ups, hello dollies, squat thrusts, push-ups, jumping jacks, and more went on for forty-five minutes. We had shed our kapok life jackets, and the yellow-accented inflatable boats were lined up and ready. A few men had already hit the tub for perceived non-performance. This was how every day started. It was usually followed by a run. Today our run would be with boats, back to the base mess hall, for a much-needed breakfast.

"It's hard to beat a person who never gives up.
Heroes get remembered, but legends never die."
—Babe Ruth

Chapter 9
Dawn Monday – Day 1

It was still ominously dark. Shadowy clouds blotted out the stars and rising sun. The biting, razor-sharp wind just would not stop. Dawn of the first full day was upon us, and with that realization, there was the welcome promise of much-needed food.

They would feed us well four times a day, and midnight rations would bring much needed calories (and mark the midpoint of one day and the countdown to the blessed dawn of another). The California sun, if it came through the clouds, would bring a new birth of hope and warmth as the countdown crept one day nearer to the end.

Breakfast, in the nearby mess hall, was a frantic and all-too-short event. We were still like deer in the headlights of an oncoming locomotive, but we ate fast and furious like our lives depended on it. It was disconcerting to find ourselves in a warm familiar military building staffed with white uniformed cooks quietly watching us. Normal warm temperatures flooded our senses in an enjoyable way. The first dawn had come, and most of us were still here.

Following this brief respite for nourishment and warmth, we were off again under our boats for the obstacle course a mile away. Some had wanted to pee, but could not take the time to go to the head (navy bathroom) since it would cut into eating time. They would pee in their boots again later.

With our boats lined up, touching bow to stern, we had a moment to savor full tummies as warmth from digesting food flowed through our veins. Some were still chewing last bits of food slipped out in pockets or hands.

"Forward, double-time march." And the boats moved out together.

One man partially regurgitated his breakfast and caught the big chunks with his covering hand. He looked at it, noticed some large chunks of egg and sausage, and gobbled it back down quickly.

"That is totally gross," noted the man next to him. He just smiled and ran on. Calories were calories, and they were *desperately* needed now.

The obstacle course was an instructor's cruel joke. We had all done this many times individually, but today we were doing it with our boats. It took forever to drag our boats up and over every obstacle, and that was the intent. Use up the day, and change shifts in the evening. Even the instructors were getting tired.

The time dragged on as boat crew after boat crew screamed, cussed, pushed, pulled and dragged their IBS by the ropes and six rubber handles. Up the cargo net thirty feet in the air, over the top, and lowered to the ground, followed by the seven men. There was confusion and failure while instructors threatened, cajoled, and brow beat individuals and teams, to move as fast as was possible. Almost an hour later, the final crew struggled around the barbed wire obstacle (not required today to save the vulnerable rubber inflatable boats) and made it to the end.

The frigidity and wind were still with us, and the instructors had everyone, except the winning boat, at leaning rest, doing push-ups with their feet up high on the boat gunwales. This made the push-ups much harder, and despite the quietly howling wind, everyone was sweating.

The last boat crew came in and joined the line of suffering push-up performers, only to hear the next event announced.

"OK Gents, the last crew is done and they will lead us back around the obstacle course. But this time you will do it backwards. This will take some imagination and leadership. You will go up the down-sloped obstacles, and down the up-sloped obstacles. However, you may skip the Slide-for-Life rope obstacle. Of course, you will take your boats with you again."

This order was a bit confusing, for we had never done something like this before, but a pattern was emerging. The instructors needed to keep us moving and off balance. Their shift would end soon, and they were looking forward to the end of their day too. This event would take just enough time to prevent another movement before the next shift arrived.

"Go, Boat Crew Seven. You dwarfs were last, and now you are first. Do *not* let the other crews pass you again. Remember, it pays to be a winner," said the instructor with a smile.

And off they all went with a loud "Hooyah," through gritted teeth.

Arms already wobbly from the leg-raised push-ups, done with boots high on the sides of the IBS, we now hoisted the boats back on our heads, and started the trek back toward the cargo net.

"OK, guys let's do it again in reverse. Three men on each side holding the side loops, and I will start up the rope with the bowline. Help me pull it upright first," directed PO2 Suter, at the request of his boat crew officer.

He had been here before and knew what to do. His last winter Hell Week attempt, in Little Creek, Virginia, was still a clear memory from almost two years ago. The BUD/S training center in Virginia was closed now. All training was centralized in Coronado.

Silver Strand Boulevard snaked alongside us, very close to the obstacle course, and as was common when it was in use, as few cars had pulled over to watch. Windows rolled down, and necks strained out to watch and hear the noises of a much-talked-about Hell Week underway. They would share their wide-eyed observations over cocktails later with friends.

Up the boat moved, and each man moved up the rope squares with it, pulling and pushing toward the telephone pole supported top. At the top, Suter, the lead man, rolled over the pole and hung onto the bowline with all his weight. The rest of the crew became pushers, instead of pullers, and over the top went the boat. Suddenly, it was falling over the other side, with only two men holding on. That was not enough manpower to prevent gravity from taking charge. The boat pulled out of their hands, and started slowly towards Suter, who was under it and looking up. His line went slack, and he reached up to stop the boat's fall. No chance of that, and the boat flew past. He realized immediately that the heavy rope that he had looped around his arm was now a great liability. The boat was going to fly by, and rip his hand or arm off.

He hooked his left leg through the twelve-inch square hole of the net and fell backwards as the boat was level with him, and in full free fall now. Hanging by the one leg, he clawed at the rope around his arm and simultaneously felt the pull increase. He started shaking his arm, and watching the loops unravel, when the line suddenly went tight with the full weight of the falling boat.

It was odd, he would later reflect, how slow time seems to move in situations like this. He could see the end result clearly, as the skin would be peeled from his arm, or his shoulder dislocated by being pulled from its socket. At the same time, he could watch the rope unravel from his arm, and he shook and swirled his arm in seemingly too slow motion.

There was a sickening *thwap* as the last loop came free of his arm and the dangling bitter end flipped back up to strike him soundly in the face. His right cheek stung like he had been slapped by a shovel, and his right eye slammed shut in pain. The boat continued its fall and bounced off the ground below. Both instructors and crewmen stood frozen in time until the boat bounced. Then everyone slowly came to life.

ENS Johnson saw what had happened, as did his crew. They were all a bit shook, so he gave a small pep talk. "Suter seems OK. You two get up there and help him down. Focus on the task here and we can avoid more injury. Help your buddy. Work together. We have a long way to go but we are ready. Get ready to move out to the next obstacle once they check Suter over."

Two men moved quickly up the rope web to help Suter down.

The corpsman was already on the move, and the crew was scrambling to help Suter now dangling by one leg. He was squinting, his right eye closed, as yellow stars flashed in his head, and he felt with his free arm, to his rope arm, searching for bone or skin ripped away. It felt numb to the touch, but the skin seemed intact as he felt for warm blood or skin bunched under his BDU sleeve. He risked a glance from his right eye, and could see the blurry helpers arrive to lift his hanging body back upright. The corpsman below was shouting orders that he could not understand, so he struggled, with help, back to a semi-sitting position with one leg through the ropes, and one leg stepping onto a rung below.

One other boat crew paused in their quest forward, and the instructors pounced, and placed them back in the leaning rest with boots on their boats. There would be a brief but unpleasant pause in the activities as a quick assessment was made.

"Are you OK?" came the corpsman's concerned voice.

"I think I am," responded Suter. The Navy had not trained him enough on these damn cargo nets, he thought as he sat there, ten feet above the ground, embarrassed and scared.

"Move slowly down the rope please," coached the corpsman.

"You men on either side, keep a hand on him until I can check is leg." He continued with real concern. He had seen this O-course do very undesirable things to people.

Suter stepped down with his good leg and then brought the other one to bear weight and was pleased to note no foot, knee, or hip pain. His right eye still stung but his vision was clearing.

"How's the arm and leg?" A light was shone shine at his pupils. Both were equal in size. Good.

"Damn, Suter! What happened to your face?"

"I think the rope hit me in the eye, but my vision seems OK now," he whispered. The rest of the crew was gathering around to see if they had lost another man.

"The rest of you get moving. You have an obstacle course to run backwards. Move out. You are holding up the game. We will send Suter back to you if he is OK," growled the instructor through his omnipresent bull horn. The other boat crews had already started up the rope ladder. The seven dwarfs were edging into the lead.

Mike looked like someone lost and confused after a bar fight. The white of his right eye was completely dark red where a small blood vessel had ruptured, and his cheek had an abrasion that looked like he had washed his cheek with a Brillo pad. But the corpsman found no other major injury. His vision checked out and a quick fundoscopic exam of the posterior eye detected no vitreous bleed. Looking through the pupil with a lighted fundoscope allowed the corpsman to assess the possibility of internal eye or retina damage. If that had been noted, a quick ambulance ride would get him to the doctor on call.

"I think he is OK to continue. I will check him again after this event," he said to the lead instructor.

"Hooyah, doc. Why don't you get him back to his crew, while I babysit these other slackers wasting my time on the ropes?"

Suter was relieved. He was also weak all over. He had taken a physical and mental beating in the last ten minutes. First, he thought he was injured, and then he thought it was over for him once again, and for the very last time, but now he was moving back to his team. His brain was still trying to understand. Did he do OK? Did he let someone down? Was it his fault, or was it just another example of *shit happens*? He was the senior enlisted man, and everyone looked to him for guidance. He needed to avoid injury at all costs, but he also needed to lead from the front. He knew what was expected of him, and he was shaken that another injury had almost done him in. He would need to be more careful.

He trotted over to his boat crew and rejoined them at the "Dirty Name" obstacle. This obstacle consisted of two levels of raised logs spaced just high enough and far apart enough that they required an aggressive jump to land, stomach first, on each log, then climb up on it, and leap to the second higher log. Short men had a very hard time with this obstacle, and cheating was commonly done by stepping on the side support beams to get a higher starting point. It was actually much *easier* now that the IBS could be angled over the top of both logs and used as a tool to pull each man up and over. Suter wisely chose to join his team as the boat was coming down. He was still shook-up, but he had avoided a few challenging obstacles while he was recovering. Every little bit helped now.

The rest of the day dragged on, and on, with more runs, surf drills, sand dune runs, and whistle drills. Instructors continued intimidating everyone, while they pushed every button they could think of. Mike found the time in the surf therapeutic for his swollen cheek and eye, but he distinctly did not like the rough waves hitting him in the back, out of an angry ocean that he was already too familiar with.

The sun rose higher, and the clouds parted. Much to our surprise, there was sunlight and warmth above us.

"Up boats!"

And six remaining boat crews hoisted the torturous inflatable rubber boats onto their heads with grunts and groans.

"Double-time, march," came the order, and off we went.

We ran *everywhere*, our feet screamed in agony, and our lungs fought for air.

"Keep those boats touching."

We scrambled to stay in line, boat touching boat, as we fought to remain in a line of bobbing black rubber, while rare onlookers shook their heads in sympathy. The onlookers were often sailors, marines, or base civilians who knew what we were doing, but had no idea why. Many had seen this before, but very few could understand why *anyone* would volunteer to undergo such obvious unpleasantness.

We arrived back at the BUD/S beach area after running along the sand dunes that lined the busy Silver Strand road which separated the BUD/S area from the Amphibious Base. Cars waited at the stoplight to watch us pass. Some cars contained currently assigned team frogmen, and our passing brought back their own memories of times like this.

"If it doesn't challenge you, it won't change you."
—Fred Devito

Chapter 10
Monday night Day 1 – back at BUD/S training center

HOURS WITHOUT SLEEP - 14
6 OFFICERS AND 33 ENLISTED

Monday late afternoon, and the sky was surprisingly bright and blue, with thin wispy clouds floating overhead on a frosty Coronado day. The sun was setting over Point Loma in the distance. Seagulls floated lazily overhead watching us and the dry beach around us. We were on the BUD/S area beach across the street from the Naval Amphibious Base, and only a few miles from the North Island Naval Air Station on the other end of the peninsula. Jets, training for their combat missions, were flying noisily overhead. Nearby locals and tourists wandered carelessly along the same beach that we were learning the taste, smell, and feel of. The landmark Hotel Del Coronado was so close we could almost see the limousines pulling up and depositing rich clientele while we sweated and shivered in their near vision. Only one road lets you onto the peninsula, where the Navy had lay claim to some of the most expensive real estate in California. Expensive private houses lined the beaches and well-laid-out streets between the Naval Air Station and Naval Amphibious base. Our sweat and blood in the sand went unnoticed.

The past hour had been spent doing relay races up and down the huge sand dune barriers put there by the Seabees (U.S. Naval Construction Battalions) and their huge beach bulldozers.

"Down boats. Stow your paddles and get upstairs to your rooms. Change into dry uniforms and be back here in ten minutes, ready to move out for dinner. Do not be late. Go."

We all sprinted as best we could to the barracks nearby, up the stairs to our rooms and shed our clothes, found dry uniforms and socks, and left the sandy mess on the floor for others to clean. The pre-trainees were there to collect the mess, sort it, wash and dry it, and have it ready if needed again, on our beds.

"Don't forget to take your vitamins," I said as we scrambled to dress. On the top shelf of each locker lay packets of vitamins sorted by the day.

"How many packets do we take now?" asked one of the crew.

"I don't know. Skip the ones with salt tabs and take the others." That was a guess on my part as I tore open three packets and looked at the mix of unidentifiable pills. I grabbed a large handful of vitamins and a protein tablet, and moved to the sink, where I gobbled what I could, in hopes that they would stay down. The rest of the crew did the same. Maybe this would help.

After the long run to the mess hall, our next meal was fast and furious. The instructors were still trying to instill fear and confusion into each moment. We arrived before normal dinner hours, and the early crew of mess specialists (meal servers) were watching in wonder as we dragged our shivering, sandy bodies through the chow line. We left a trail of sand on their nice waxed linoleum floors, since during the run here, instructors had found some beach to roll around in. Kapok life jackets and paddles lay neatly where we had placed them on our boats outside.

After a very appreciated moment of calm spent stuffing every available calorie into our system, we were back outside amid yelling and screaming and whistles directing us in multiple directions. Chaos tried to reign. One man regurgitated and, once again, instantly tried to gobble up what was on his clothes or in his hands. The food was essential to survival. No one even noticed this time.

"Line up the boats. Tighten the gaps. Now, double-time march," hollered the corpsman tasked with bringing us back to the BUD/S area for our next event.

We were told that our next task was back at the BUD/S beach area, where we had spent our first few hours. Now we lined up again to run back where we came from. The logistics failed to make sense unless you realized that the real goal was *exhaustion*.

"Log PT is next. Down boats," came the order once we arrived at the beach.

Our boat crews had been adjusted to ensure that at least six men remained under each boat. Our numbers were already dwindling. In front of the line of downed boats waited the heavy, pitch-covered telephone poles that we had practiced with during this first phase of training. We lined up by boat crew alongside our six logs and waited.

"Sit-ups," came the command.

And we lay our logs on our chests and began to count out the exercises in unison. Twenty sit-ups done in unison, and we found ourselves standing up, as ordered, with the hateful poles held a full arm's length above our heads. Shoulder muscles burned, and arms shook, as we struggled once again to push against gravity. Groans were heard as instructors circled looking for slackers.

"Rosensweig, you short little Mexican *buttwipe*. You are not doing your share. Drop for push-ups." Suddenly, the log was heavier for the remaining men. They groaned in unison.

"Do you think this is a time to rest? Do you want your teammates to carry your load?" he screamed while kicking sand in Rosy's face.

"No, Instructor Rogers," was all he could choke out as he closed his eyes to avoid the beach being thrown in his face. His mouth was full of beach grit as he sucked air to survive.

"Then recover and help your boat crew. They need you, and you need them. Am I clear?" Chief Rogers was intimidating. His muscles seemed to have muscles.

"Yes, Chief," choked Rosy as he and resumed his place under the hateful burden. He feared failure, but he was more fearful of being viewed as a slacker. He pushed up as hard as he could, and lessened the burden for all.

"Take your logs to the surf zone and line up behind them facing the beach, then have a seat behind them. It is time for a race, and folks, it pays to be a winner."

All six crews moved together and placed their logs in the froth. The race was explained – on the start signal each crew must push their log up the incline of the beach back to the starting point of soft sand now fifty feet away. The line of instructors waited on top of the small hill.

The bullhorn bellowed, and on command, each man pushed with his legs while holding position with their hands in the surf behind them. One foot at a time, the logs moved up the uncooperative beach. When one man failed to push in unison the log shifted right or left. This was an exercise in teamwork. The dwarfs were winning. They still had not lost a man. *Guts* was their mantra, and they worked well together. Shorter legs seemed to work better in unison.

Commands given by each boat crew leader echoed in the morning breezes, and the logs moved slowly up the incline. One crew was unable to get their log to move in a straight line, and the instructors pounced.

"Mr. Fields, you pile of stinking whale droppings, get your team organized. Move this log together." He began shoveling the beach onto each crew member. The additional harassment did nothing to help.

The dwarf crew won easily and was ordered to sit quietly on their log and watch the chaos below. They were respectfully quiet as they paused and panted in unison to regain lost energy.

The bullhorn blared insults and encouragement. The beach fought back and the logs moved slowly forward. As Mr. Fields' crew failed again to operate as a team, their log continued to move right and left. The instructors ordered them to return to the surf zone in disgrace. This time the boat's senior NCO, Tom Valentine, would give the commands, as instructed, with a greater focus born from failure, and Tom's carefully timed commands, the log moved effectively up the beach.

ENS Fields was now being watched.

Radioman Second Class (RM2) Tom Valentine had been the second of four children growing up in a rough part of Pennsylvania, and he had been in his first semester at Lehigh University when the last of the Vietnam

War draft took place. His draft number was 3, and the draft board advised him that he would be called up. Student deferments had been done away with. He had no real desire to go into the military, but after examining his options, he had decided to enlist in the Navy for a few years, and then get back to his studies later.

Life had been interesting for Tom as a boy, but he had endured a troublesome time reconciling his parents' breakup. Tom took his mother's side, a choice that resulted in conflict with his father. The conflict became physical and often ended up in fights on the front yard. He focused his energies on Boy Scouts instead, where he enjoyed the challenge and opportunity. Tom became an Eagle Scout and earned Order of the Arrow awards. He had been tested as an individual. Scouting had given him the opportunity to show others that he was OK. His parents' problems were not his fault.

He was fit and handsome with an intelligence that he used in all his individual pursuits. He and his younger brother had hitchhiked twenty-five miles to Bishop Egan Catholic high school, and back, each day. The Navy offered Tom a new challenge and opportunity.

After another knockdown, drag-out fist fight with his father, he decided that the Navy would bring him happier times. He left for San Diego Boot Camp shortly thereafter. A few months later, Kathy, his high school sweetheart, and girl next door, accepted his marriage proposal.

She made him wait until she was nineteen to wed. They would be poor, but travel and adventure awaited. Tom was handsome, fit, and quietly independent. She loved him the moment they met while ice skating on the Delaware Canal at age fifteen. He was the first man she had ever kissed, it was on 28 February, and it was magical. They celebrate that anniversary to this day.

Tom had quickly figured out that their futures were intertwined, and it proved to be a good decision, asking her to marry him. She was by his side each day of training, ironing his uniform, polishing his shoes, and feeding him quickly before cuddling up to him in bed. This made training more tolerable. Failure here meant going to the fleet with the prospect of long deployments at sea. Tom and Kathy both knew this. Quitting was not an option.

The afternoon sun was setting and not providing much heat. The air was wintry and crisp. A damp salty smell was in the air as breezes blew the nautical smells of seaweed and tar from the bay behind us to the ocean to the west. The bay was marred with piers of grey Navy ships tied quietly alongside. Their white numerals painted brightly on the bows designated them as submarine tenders, destroyer escorts, and amphibious ships. They would serve as targets later in training when we planted magnetic mines to their hulls during diving exercises. These smells would change at night when the temperatures dropped. At night, the prevailing winds came from the ocean to the land as the land cooled and drew the sea air in. This made the nights *much* worse to endure, as the intense cold was infused with the penetrating, wet, salt air of the Pacific Ocean.

"Drop, Mr. Muggs, you slimy piece of horse dung. Give me fifty more." Another order mixed in with the cacophony of yelling and cajoling going on all around.

The wide white stripe on his fiberglass helmet was scuffed through the white and the base green color to the brown fiberglass underneath. It identified him as an officer, so his moniker began with "Mister" when the instructor issued his commands. He was one of many in the leaning rest position. His boat crew and he had their feet resting on the main tube of their IBS. This made the feet higher than the head and made push-ups significantly more difficult.

But his arms would not work anymore. They were numbed from the bitter chill, and his mind was foggy from lack of sleep. He was concerned but determined.

However, fear is a superb motivator. He had not developed much new muscle yet, but that would come in time. His boxing background had served him well so far. He had powerfully developed arms.

Fifty more push-ups seemed impossible.

He had been looking forward to Hell Week since he first learned about it at the Naval Academy. This would be a personal challenge beyond anything he had ever endured, and as a boxer, he had endured much. He wanted to find his true limit. He wanted to suffer as never before. And he had known plenty of physical and psychological pain and suffering in the past.

As a Naval Academy graduate, he had made it through a difficult academic year while also memorizing the entire "plebe" (freshmen) minutia required in the Reef Points book. Everyone learned how to polish shoes, wear various uniforms, make a bed properly, and obey orders given by upperclassmen who seemed to enjoy making life difficult. They had formations for all three meals a day, and lights out happened at 1030 PM, ready or not. Push-ups and uniform changing drills were saved for after class and weekends. Sometimes this seemed to be just for the amusement of upperclassmen who had endured the same before.

He had never enjoyed other people's pain, and he never willingly inflicted any on the plebes he was later responsible for. He broke fewer rules than most. He got caught sometimes, and marched hours of penalty tours with a rifle, marching after class on Wednesday and Friday and sometimes on weekends.

That was mild harassment compared to what was ahead, but it had taught him that it was not personal. It was part of the test, and the test was simply a game that others played. Often they failed to explain the rules. That had turned out to be good preparation for the unknown elements of this training.

And now he was looking at fifty more push-ups and he wondered how that could be asked of him again. The sparkling sand on his face was itching where the unrelenting wind was drying it. The grit in his crotch had worn his groin raw where the prohibited underwear might have been. The fiberglass green helmet was stenciled with MUGGS on the front. The top was worn to rough brown fiberglass. His chin was raw from the strap holding it askew, but in place. Sweat dripped unnoticed, like drips from an icicle, from his frosty, cherry-red nose. This was both horrifying and exciting. He wanted to do this, he needed to find his limit, but he was afraid. He could not stop. He had to go on. He knew he could, but he did not know if there was a yet undiscovered place where pain, or cold, or exhaustion, would beat him.

"Goddamn it, sir, you will perform or you will quit! Are you a quitter?" screamed the animated instructor as he kicked pile after nasty pile of sand into his face, mouth, and neck. He felt it weighing him down, as it collected between his chest and wet undershirt, like an iron anvil. The weight was aggravating and frustrating, and he imagined it as contributing to his current self-inflicted dilemma. Fatigue was affecting his thinking. Focus on the task at hand was all he was capable of. His conscious mind was focused only on this task. His unconscious mind was screaming that he had endured worse before and not to stop. *Not now, not ever.* The clock was ticking slowly through another day of windy chill, and penetrating wet. Thoughts about this ending must not enter his mind.

Is this still the first day? Did the sun come up again, or is it going to set soon?
Either way, it did not matter, so he did the fifty more push-ups.

"You must never confuse faith that you will prevail in the end – which you can never afford to lose – with the discipline to confront the most brutal facts of your current reality, whatever they might be.
—VADM James Stockdale

Chapter 11
Tuesday dawn Day 2 – Amphibious base track field

HOURS WITHOUT SLEEP - 30
6 OFFICERS AND 31 ENLISTED - 2 HAD QUIT
DURING THE NIGHT

He needed to do more push-ups now. They all did, or so the instructor had ordered. The class was spread out on the grassy field surrounded by the dark, quarter mile running track.

Physics had been a favorite subject in high school, and the laws Petty Officer Winget had studied were universally absolute. Force equals mass times acceleration. Power is the amount of energy consumed over time. Energy can be used to do work, and work requires movement. Those were some of the undeniable laws of the universe. Holding his arms in the leaning rest position caused pain and effort, but work began only with movement. Leaning rest was a painful place to be with arms straight, back straight, and wet boot toes in the sand. His plan was to avoid movement, and thus avoid work. Each push-up needed to allow enough movement in the arms to appear as enough to qualify as a real push-up, but avoid going so far that getting back up required an unobtainable extra effort. Work must be conserved.

He had it figured out in his mind. The well-trained instructor knew the game too well, and he watched him and the other trainees carefully. He would allow some slack if the effort appeared real enough, so grunting and loud breathing were essential to the effort, if it was to be believed. Grunting and strained huffing or puffing required less work than an actual push-up. If the instructor were to glance away and timing was just right, a push-up or two could be counted aloud with only minimal movement. This was a game of survival. He wanted to survive. He looked forward to the pain in a curious way. He needed vindication from his previous quit during his last Hell Week. He already held the class record for the fastest obstacle course time by using experience, ability, and physics to his advantage.

"One, sir, two, sir," he groaned dramatically. And the adrenalin-aided unachievable happened again. His arms worked again, and he was grateful. They clearly should not work any longer. Not after all they had just done – far beyond what had ever been asked of these muscles and tendons and joints. In the past, track competitions with demanding coaches, had taught him about physical limits. He thought he knew what those limits were.

He was seriously misinformed – we *all* were – and this was just the beginning. He had not slept for almost two days now, and memories of his previous BUD/S training flooded over him. This was the same day in a past Hell Week that an officer in his previous class had encouraged him to quit. The memory haunted him. He finished the task with resolve and moved back to his boat crew who were waiting in a leaning rest position, with feet raised onto the boat gunnel.

"Recover," ordered the instructor, and they all rose slowly. The instructor moved to the next crew where a thin and focused sailor was pushing out his push-ups, but was counting too slow.

"You sorry excuse for a tadpole, if you do not get your ass moving I am going to have every swinging dick here hit the bay again," he screamed, as Tom Hanrath, AKA *the mighty mosquito*, paused his push-ups in exhaustion.

"Nineteen sir, twenty sir," he counted as he looked straight ahead, holding a shaking leaning rest position. His arms and back muscles screamed at him, and he thought agonizingly of causing the unthinkable to happen to his class.

It was winter, and the icy Pacific Ocean nearby is especially unforgiving this time of the year.

Tom was not completely in control of his own thoughts. The mission at hand was important, the next hot and greatly-needed meal was too far away, and the nameless shadow of his tormentor wobbled in his current consciousness. He cared about this excruciating moment in time but was resigned to the discovery of limits anxiously awaited and yet to be fully experienced. This was an expected part of a long-awaited for week. He knew that, if he finished, his dream job awaited him. The numbing iciness all around was mildly irrelevant, but omnipresent. He knew he would try until he could not try anymore. There was only this moment in his mind. One push-up at a time was all that was required. To think further into the future would be a recipe for doubt. Doubt is a dangerous emotion that often leads to failure. But not now, not *ever* would he consider quitting. Death was a preferable outcome.

It was Tuesday morning now, he thought. Time lacked a reliable point of reference.

We were all starving, like ravenous rats anxious to eat the dead. This was a state we seemed to be aware of only when there was time to think about it. Hunger would usually kick in again only one hour after filling each of us with as much food as our stomachs could hold.

The class was spread out on the soccer field facing Glorietta Bay. We were now lying flat in the grass fighting to keep our eyes open. The sun was rising in the east. The game now was to see who fell asleep.

"Rosensweig, you lazy, wet-back spic, hit the bay. You are failing to follow commands. You are asleep on duty. We hung sailors for that in the past."

Rosy jumped up, shook off the fog of much needed sleep, waited for his swim buddy to reluctantly join him, and they trotted to the bay together, climbed carefully over the rock wall and splashed into the reviving waters. The instructor followed and waited while his charges got cold enough.

"Recover assholes. Get your butts back on the grass and count to one hundred out loud.

They climbed out together, as two other men climbed reluctantly into the water, followed by their own tormentor.

Another swim pair was ordered to the bay. It was Don Sayre and his current swim buddy. Don had lost his first buddy during rock portage the first night, and his new buddy was having trouble keeping up. Don was a superb swimmer and a good runner. As they moved to the water his partner tripped and fell forward knocking Don down. The instructors attacked.

"Sayre, you are not helping your buddy. Is he a *problem* for you?" said the nearest instructor.

"No, Instructor Thornton. We are a team," he said.

"Then get in the water now."

"Hooyah, Instructor Thornton," he replied and leapt over the slippery boulders into the flat bay waters. His swim buddy was still trying to see if he was hurt, and he failed to follow.

Splash went Don, and when he looked around, his swim buddy was missing.

Oh crap, he thought as scrambled back up the rocks to his buddy.

Too late.

"Sayre, you idiot. You left your buddy behind. In combat, he would be dead. How will you explain that to his family?"

He reached down and helped up his charge knowing he was in trouble. They started to move together to the bay hoping for the best.

"Nice try, Gentlemen. Go back to the medical truck and find the buddy hawser in there. Tie it around your waists and get back here now."

This was bad. The hawser was a three-inch thick rope used to moor ships to the pier. It was *very* heavy, ten feet long, and cumbersome. Everyone had been threatened with this punishment if they failed to stay together.

His buddy groaned, and he looked to Sayre for help out of this mess. There was no way out, so up to the truck they trotted and found the hawser. The corpsman helped them tie it around their soggy waists, and back to the beach they went. The hawser dragged on the gravel between them and walking was difficult.

Splash, splash – and they were in the bay again. The heavy rope pulled down on them both.

"I can't do this, Don," whispered his partner with wide eyes as he spit out saltwater.

"Yes, you can. We both can. Hang in there, buddy," Don said.

"No, I really can't. I am not sure I want to anymore."

The instructors watched with interest, but ordered them out of the bay.

"Drop for push-ups, Gentlemen," came the next order, and Don dropped to a leaning rest. His buddy just stood there.

"Get down here, please," said Don, but his plea fell on deaf ears.

To his horror, he watched his buddy untie the hawser and start up the field toward the truck coldly displaying the brass bell.

He jumped up, followed. "Don't do this, we can do this. Look how far we have come. It is only a few more days and we are done."

The instructors followed silently. This would be a test for both men.

"Don, I am sorry," he whispered. "I want to go home. I want to be warm again. There are other places I can go."

"Instructor Thornton, I am done. I am holding Sayre back, and I have had enough."

Thornton looked at Don who was wide-eyed in disbelief and shock. He was failing his buddy. He was witness to the unthinkable again.

"Sayre, stand fast. I want to speak with this man in private," and they stepped away together. Don just stood there holding the heavy hawser tied around his waist only.

"Are you *sure* you are done? Do you want to quit? Do you realize that there is no second chance here?" asked Frisk. Instructor Thornton was tall and caring, and intense. He took every lost trainee personally. He had taken this job because he believed in the Teams and the future it held for him, and his teammates.

"I am sure, Instructor."

"Well then, let's go get you some hot chocolate and a blanket," he said loud enough for Sayre to hear. Sometimes when one man quit, another would follow.

"Sayre, you have failed again. Your swim buddy is leaving you again. Don't you think you should join him for hot chocolate and a blanket?" he challenged.

"No thank you, Instructor," was all he could muster.

"Then get your disappointing ass over to Instructor Tyvdik and ask for another swim buddy. You can leave the hawser here for now."

The two men moved to the truck, and three rings of the ever-present, shiny brass bell echoed across the field, marking the loss of his classmate. To ring the bell was a final insult to endure once a man called it quits. The bell would ring three times with an instructor witness, and the helmet would be placed in line, back at the BUD/S area, with the others already there.

He had other places he could go and feel good about himself.

Don moved on as directed. He had mixed feelings. Only minutes ago, they were fighting to survive together. They had promised to support each other, no matter what. Now he was moving on, temporarily feeling alone. The name of his swim buddy was already fading. In a week, he would have trouble remembering his name or face. In a month, his place in Don's memory would be gone forever.

NAB Coronado on the right on Glorietta Bay, BUD/S area on the left Pacific Ocean
beach side

Instructor Tyvdik during Hell Week; none of these men graduated with the class

Instructor Frisk oversees rock portage training

Rock Portage training – Only one finished with the class

Lined up for inspection at "Beautiful Mud Haven by the Bay"

Stuck in the mud

Digging for clams – yummy

Medical Inspection with wooden guns

ENS Adams Graduation day

Graduation Day – RM2 Tom Valentine

Graduation Day – PN2 Mike Suter

FIRST ROW – ENS Randy Albracht, ATAN Tom Hanrath, SA Bob McNabb, RM2 Tom
Valentine, ENS Robert Adams
SECOND ROW – SA David Hyman, FTG3 Frank Winget, SA Don Sayre, PN2 Mike Suter,
MM3 David Banton, ENS John Muggs (pseudonym)

CDR Adams the day he was sworn in as an Army 2LT to attend medical school

Eleven still standing at graduation

The Commanding Officer
Naval Amphibious School, Coronado
requests the pleasure of your company
at the Graduation Ceremony for
Basic Underwater Demolition Seal Training
Class Eightyone
the 4th day of April One Thirty P.M.
Building 604
Naval Amphibious Base
Coronado, California

Uniform
Reception Follows   *Participants: Service Dress Blue*
Building 604   *Guests: Uniform of the Day*

Graduation Invitation

Ten of the eleven return 30 years later with Instructors Steve Frisk and Mike Thornton

Mike Thornton presented the class with his Medal of Honor coin noting:

"This was the best SEAL class I ever put through training!"

"If you're going through hell, keep going."
—Winston Churchill

Chapter 12
Tuesday morning – Day 2

HOURS WITHOUT SLEEP - 34
6 OFFICERS AND 30 ENLISTED

Evening meal had been a luxurious event. It occurred at the Coronado Naval Amphibious base mess hall. We had run, slipped, and stumbled the necessary painful and grueling miles to get there, with our omnipresent rubber boats painfully bouncing on our heads. Tonight, it would be unheated MREs (Meals Ready to Eat) and it would be difficult to open the cans of gelatinous meat, with the tiny one-and-a-half-inch folding P-38 "John Wayne" can openers provided, since our cold fingers would be weak, numb, and shaking from the near polar air.

This morning, however, we were moving in a trance through the food line. There was no wind. The room was pleasantly heated, and the awed and sympathetic mess cooks would pile as much food as our plates could hold onto our trays. There was hot coffee and hot chocolate that smelled like heaven – as we imagined it– and we would dip our shivering sandy hands into the scalding liquid to warm them, drinking it, sand and all, while we went slowly through the line in a calorie-deprived daze. Brain function slows with cold, but it slows exceedingly fast when there is no sugar to feed the main control centers. The brain can only use sugar for fuel. It must direct the conversion of protein and fat to sugar by the liver and other organs, which is a longer, more complicated physiologic process. Before the conversion happens, it will take stored sugars from the muscles. Once the muscle stores are gone, and the conversion process begins, there is a period of cellular starvation. Now the process of generating heat through shivering lessens due to lack of fuel, the brain starts to shut down unnecessary functions – like analytic thinking – and the brainstem gets the available calories to maintain automatic functions like heartbeat, breathing, and digestion. We know instinctively what needs to be done, and we force each step forward as a survival thought kicks in – *Eat!*

This was a blessed thirty minutes of food and heat, while instructors circled to ensure we ate, and did not fall asleep. A missed meal would be a disaster. This training burned calories at a rate known nowhere else in the world. We were all losing weight and destroying muscles at the same time. Once the immediately available calories were gone, the body would seek calories from the muscle stores. This was a physiologic phenomenon that caused iron deficiency anemia, renal failure, congestive heart strain, and mental confusion. The sugar levels could drop so low that the brain would not function properly. Our core body temperatures were dropping, and they were now below ninety degrees much of the time. This affected muscle and brain function. The master control panel was overloaded, and the needed fuel was low.

Tom Hanrath was falling asleep next to me. His hand was paused half way to his mouth. I elbowed him to eat. He tried again and got a chunk of pancake dripping in much needed syrup to his mouth. I was suspicious that he had fallen asleep at the last midnight meal and that we had failed to wake him.

"Chew it," I said quietly, not wanting attention from the instructors yet. His swim buddy looked worried too.

Tom was the smallest man in our class, but maybe the toughest. He was a terrifying five feet six inches tall and weighed an insignificant 135 pounds soaking wet. He had no body fat at all, and his muscles were lean and taught from years of competitive spring board diving. The instructors called him the mighty mosquito. He *needed* this food. His tray was full to overflowing, but it was not making it to his mouth.

Tom grew up in small town in Marshfield, Wisconsin, in the middle of an icy, almost arctic nowhere. The Navy had been a way out of a place where he did not want to be.

His father was his own school's principal and the superintendent of schools. Tom was an underachiever in school, per his demanding parents, and he took a job as a truck driver on graduation. It was not his idea of success. He went to the military recruiters, and the Army offered him a job as a tank driver. This was too close to what he had been trying to escape. The Navy had said aviation electronics was available, based on his good scores. This was a career option that could lead to a job with the airlines. They looked at his gaunt body and failed to even mention Navy Special Forces. That was clearly not an option.

His dad was an alcoholic, an overachiever, and the only child of nine who had earned a college degree. His father was violent and had never said he was proud of him – even when he achieved class president, karate stud, and track star. Never hugged as a child, his parents had never expected him to achieve anything.

His sister, with a genius IQ, had no love to share, and his brother, with an almost photographic memory, forced him to be a rebel trying to beat the system. He was the third of four children, with the last brother arriving seven years after he did. He was almost invisible.

Discipline for Tom was to stay home as punishment while his brother was sent outside to play for similar offenses. He rebelled to get noticed, and it rarely resulted in the love he sought.

He chose the Navy electronics option, and was assigned to VR-21 in Barbers Point Hawaii, as an aviation electronics tech. It was a unit with C-118 prop planes and two C-130 combat transports, but these planes had very few electronics, so he was not challenged by much.

All-Navy spring board diving champion was his only claim to fame so far, but his dad still seemed unimpressed. He had not called him once since joining the Navy. Tom had been a good diver in high school, and he loved the water. When the Navy told him that there was a diving team he could join, and compete on, he signed up immediately. Even better, that gave him time off to practice and go to meets. So far, the Navy was not such a bad idea, but he wanted more.

Richard Widmark, in the 1951 film *The Frogmen* had been his childhood idol – the film was a World War II story about the U.S. Navy's underwater demolition units, the frogmen. He had watched it too many times to remember. "Fin-footed, goggle eyed, beach blasting heroes" read the movie summary. This led him to consider other options.

His friend Scott had just failed to complete BUD/S but had told him that he had not wanted it enough. Boredom and an easy job for one more year in his Hawaii assignment gave Tom time to run, and run, and run. It allowed him to meet other SEALs – and *future* SEALs – so he decided to *want it* more than Scott had.

He jumped the chain link fence to the chief's pool and worked out in the evenings to ready him for what he knew he wanted to do. BUD/S was going to be in his future, he was sure. But the morning of day two found that reality in jeopardy.

We were all in desperate need of calories and the heat they can generate. I stuffed more food into me, all mixed together and flavorless, while I watched Tom out of the corner of my eye. Our goal was to fill the constantly empty tanks to maximum, and then add a little bit more. Meals earlier had tried desperately to regurgitate in revenge as we ran on to the next evolution, but we could not let that happen. Nasty and acidic, we would all re-chew the critically needed morsels and swallow them gratefully once more. By now, we were learning that we needed lots and lots of calories. Hunger was not a big issue. Obtaining enough fuel to last until the next meal *was*. Our food would be backed up from stomach to esophagus, with periodic swallowing needed just to keep it there. Yet, we knew that, one hour later, gnawing hunger grumblings would begin again.

Tom Hanrath was starting to seriously worry about his swim buddy. He would not swallow. His eyes were open, and he nodded to our words, but I was sure he was asleep or in a state like sleep. I would learn later that he was *severely* hypoglycemic, and the human brain without nutrients does not work well.

"On your feet, Gentlemen. To your boats, now," screamed the always watchful instructors.

"Hooyahaaaaaah," we replied hoarsely, and as one we rose to limp, shuffle, or slide to our rubber boats, waiting and guarded by a classmate outside.

Wet sand marked our paths on seats and floor as we ambled out. Tom did not move from his seat despite my insistent urging.

An instructor finally saw his swim buddy trying to help Tom, and came over.

"Corpsman!" he called firmly, as he told us both to move on. I hesitated and he was more direct.

"Move it, you two. We will handle this," he said firmly but kindly, as the corpsman walked knowingly over with his omnipresent medical bag in hand. Hypothermia and exhaustion were familiar maladies. He knew what to do.

We both reluctantly left Tom. He was an inspiration to me, and his partner was suddenly alone needing a reassignment to another swim buddy. Tom probably should not have made it this far. He was thin, like the competitive diver he was, and thus had very little stored fat in reserve.

At our last four-mile timed beach run, I had been praying out loud to make the thirty-two-minute time cut, and with the end in sight, I heard Tom coming up beside me praying the same words. "Please God," he whispered, "just help me to make it again this time."

They were the same words I was whispering aloud, and we both realized it. He reached out and grabbed my hand as we ran the final yards to the finish line. It looked like we were finishing the Olympic marathon, as teammates tied for first place, but we were well fed and warm then.

Now, I was sure I had lost another classmate.

The corpsman did a quick assessment as we all filed out. Tom responded slowly to his questions with glazed eyes. His movements were slow and labored like he was moving through a vat of Jell-O. This was something he had seen before.

"Get the ambulance driver in here," the corpsman stated loudly. "I need to start an IV and get this man to the clinic. He has hypoglycemia, hypothermia, and possible dehydration." He pulled out a liter of five percent glucose solution in a bag preloaded with tubing and IV needle. Before the ambulance driver arrived, he had already neatly, and perfectly, inserted the large twenty-two-gauge needle into Tom's right arm vein, and was covering it with a transparent plastic protective Op-site cover, while another instructor stood by holding the bag in the air. It was running the sugar fluid in at full tilt.

"I have the litter," the driver said calmly. "Let's load and transport. The doc at the clinic is aware that we are en route. I radioed ahead"

Tom arrived at the BUD/S medical facility six minutes later in the ambulance with lights flashing. LCDR Christianson, MD, DMO, was waiting outside his office. He had seen this before and was sure this was another casualty that would not be returning, but much to his displeasure, he knew they would likely give him the option of returning.

A rapid but complete exam noted that he was hypothermic with a rectal temperature of 91 degrees. Not good. His resting heart rate was fast at 145 and blood pressure was low at 105/55. He was responsive, but seemed confused. He was asking to go back with his class.

"Mr. Hanrath, take a few minutes here please while we determine if you are OK," stated the doctor professionally while putting his stethoscope in his ears. The IV was almost empty now, so he ordered another one to be warmed in the microwave and hung next. Tom was already wrapped in a Navy issued wool blanket and oven-warmed bean bags were being placed in his groin and armpits by the corpsmen. They all knew what to do. This was a frequent problem after days without sleep, exposed to icy water and air constantly. If it weren't for the regular large quantity of food, and constant activity, every single trainee would be on a table with an IV right now.

As the warmed glucose solution began to flow in, Tom began to shiver. He had been too bone chilled to shiver before. The corpsmen added another blanket. After only two hours, with Tom fast asleep, the first phase officer LT Scotty Lyons, and the proctor Chief Puckett came in.

"Tom, you gave it a great try, and we will absolutely consider you for rollback to another class later, but I think you will agree that Hell Week is over now?"

"No sir. I feel much better now. I have eaten some protein bars and stopped shivering, and I want to return to my class please, sir."

He looked almost panicked and was glancing around at the whole collection of corpsmen and staff shaking their heads in relative disbelief. It was still severely crisp out there, and he would have to put back on a wet uniform, they thought, to join his class now en route to the dreaded mud flats.

The officer looked at his watch and calculated where the rest of the class would be now. They were paddling the Pacific Ocean toward the Mexican border. He knew that this thin, frail appearing man would most likely never make it another day in the Siberian cold and wet ahead, but policy did allow him to try.

"Chief, I think he's nuts, but I admire his drive. Get him in a dry uniform and boots, and *drive* him to the mud flats."

Turning to Tom with visible compassion and admiration in his eyes, the doc said, "Good luck, sailor. God bless."

> "Greatness is not achieved by never falling
> but by rising each time we fall."
> —Confucius

Chapter 13
To the mud flats. Tuesday afternoon – Day 2

HOURS WITHOUT SLEEP - 40
6 OFFICERS AND 29 ENLISTED
(TOM IS IN THE SICK BAY CLINIC)

While Tom was in the clinic, the class had run on wet, swollen feet to the BUD/S compound and was ordered to paddle their boats to Mexico. Well, not all the way there, but almost. The mud flats awaited them for the next couple days. The flats were located just north of the Mexico border, and were inhabited only by bugs, clams, and birds. The smell of the mud on low tide could gag a vulture; even in 1974/75 there was a great deal of raw Tijuana sewage discharged into the Tijuana River.

The six remaining boat crews lined up next to the large sand dunes for a mission brief. Our last meal was still packed in our stomachs, and we were all freshly wet from team tumbling acrobatics in the surf. It was time to head south, our instructors said, for some fun in the mud.

The surf was a bit concerning, with three-foot cruncher coming in at a slight angle. The instructors were discussing how to start the race to the Mexico border. A decision was made to keep it fair. Some instructors had developed their favorite crews already, and some beer bets were at stake.

My boat crew had won all the boat races on the water so far, but we had lost some sand dune races to the lighter, faster crews. The seven dwarfs were all together still, and doing well. It was rumored that one crew would be secured early, and if that was true, we all wanted it to be *our* crew.

"Here are the rules. Each boat must pass through the surf and dump boat. Once you have completed an approved dump boat dump drill you will assemble in line just past the breakers. Once we see all boats lined up we will signal the start with an air horn," stated Instructor Joe Tyvdik through the hand-held bullhorn.

"The finish line will be marked with a MK-13 smoke flare and a white flag on a pole. Report your boat to the instructor on the beach when you arrive. Remember, winning is good. You may all begin now. Go."

The first boat, commanded by ENS Fields, hit the waves, flipped sideways, and all seven men were washed back to the shallows. The other boats saw this and waited for the right time to attack the waves. It was best to wait for the wave to break, and then paddle as fast as possible through the froth before the next line of waves hit, and tossed us all in the air like a cork.

Three boats tried to breach past the breakers at the same time. ENS Muggs's boat and my boat made it with only seconds to spare before getting hit by the next wave. ENS Albracht, who was born and raised in Iowa, far from the waves, had waited for us to make a move before following. This cost him the few seconds he needed, and his boat got caught sideways, and was washed ignominiously back towards shore. They did not flip, but the Zodiac was full of seawater so they had to walk it back to the shallows and dump boat, reload, and try again. An instructor watching seemed happy with the failure. Most likely, he had just won a beer bet.

The first two boats safely past the surf line dutifully grabbed the side ropes, leaned back, and pulled the boat upside down. The fast crewmen could scramble up and over the boat as it flipped, and remain relatively dry, on top of the now inverted boat. With the other four crewmen now treading water, and kept afloat by their kapok life jackets, the top men repeated the dump boat procedure, in reverse, and righted the boat, while at the same time, pulling three men, holding onto the side handles, into the boat. The coxswain climbed in the back with assistance.

Dump boat drills accomplished, the crews starting hand bailing the water in their boats. Every pound of water would slow them, and it paid to be a winner. Then, one by one, the other boats made it through the waves and lined up in the wind and spray waiting for the starting horn. There was some grumbling and yelling as some boat crews seemed to be happier than others.

The horn blared long and loud.

"All pull together," came the six coxswain's commands simultaneously, as had been practiced so many times before. The race began. It made no sense to push too hard. We had a few hours of paddling ahead. Slow and steady was the plan, and the big guys of Boat One started to pull ahead.

It seemed that our boat pre-preparation was paying off. Unannounced to the other boat crews, we had borrowed an extra inflatable bottom from an unused IBS. This made our boat a touch heavier, but our theory was that we would float higher and have less resistance in the water. In addition, we had purchased spray silicone, and coated the entire bottom and side of the boat with it to make resistance less. It seemed to work.

We had always planned to win, as did each crew. We had also found a nutrition expert and had asked her to help us formulate a vitamin and supplement plan to help battle the nutritional demands of muscle fatigue, cold, and endurance. She had helped us assemble three packets per day to be taken with each meal. This was a great idea in theory, but since we rarely made it back to the barracks, the vitamin packets were mostly untouched in our lockers. However, there were a few opportunities where we made it to our lockers, on instructor orders, to change clothes. In those moments, we would all grab two or three vitamin packs and scarf them down at the sink or water fountain. We all thought this would help, and as I look back, I am certain that it did.

It is worth commenting that, over the years, nutrition has taken a greater importance as knowledge has increased in this area. Additionally, performance-enhancing supplements have become popular for athletes. Unfortunately, some supplements are just plain dangerous in an endurance event. In response to a supplement-related death from congestive heart failure, caused by supplements used by a trainee during Hell Week some years ago, the training now bans all supplements. A trainee must sign an agreement that he will not use supplements except for one multivitamin provided daily by the medical personnel. In addition, they are banned from going to Mexico where injectable steroids and supplements are available with ease. This has undoubtedly saved lives.

Our boat held a commanding lead as we neared the finish. The instructor ashore pulled the ring on his MK-13 orange smoke flare. We'd won and were directed to take a break on the beach while we waited for the others. This was heavenly. The sun was shining, and only our legs and boots were seriously wet from dragging the boat ashore.

Each subsequent boat that arrived was declared a loser and ordered to perform another dump boat drill before joining us on the shore. Once all the crews were assembled, and a few encouraging or disparaging words were exchanged among crews, we were marched, with boats once again bouncing off our helmets, to the trucks waiting for us on higher ground. The stench of the mud flats assaulted us immediately.

There was activity at the instructor vehicles as a lighted vehicle pulled up. A red cross was visible on the side, and the back doors opened. Two men emerged and moved to a roaring fire. One was dressed like an instructor, and the other was dressed like the rest of us. We all squinted to see who it was, but could not make out a face – but he was short and lean, and he was being directed to move to one of the other boat crews.

Wat that *Tom*, back from the dead? Maybe we have not lost him after all. We could hardly believe it.

A fresh replacement instructor came over to my boat crew. They changed shifts every eight hours. We were still seven men. Some boat crews were down to five or six, as some of their members had chosen to quit. One more officer had elected to ring the bell and we were down to five officers.

I asked if it was Tom in the ambulance, and was told it was.

"Is he OK?" I asked incredulously. "He's back. That is all you need to know."

> "More men fail though lack of purpose
> than lack of talent."
> —Bill Sunday

Chapter 14
Tuesday Evening Day 2

HOURS WITHOUT SLEEP - 48
5 OFFICERS AND 29 ENLISTED

"Listen up. We are going to be here for a while, Gents, so we need tents. Everyone grab a pup tent and get to work setting it up in a nice straight row. Two men per tent, so your swim buddy is your bunk mate. We are going to build another beautiful Mud City by the Bay. We all moved quickly to the task, and we soon had a nice double line of enticing shelters facing each other and ready to go. We were covered with muck and slime and had not slept in days. The thought of a nap was intoxicating. The muck all over us had come from a long series of relay races in the river of mud just below us. Tom was back, and his boat crew had six men again.

"Respectable job, Gentlemen. We are going to take a nap now, but for security purposes you will need a roving security watch. That watch will change every five minutes. If you are on watch, you will walk back and forth between the tents you are guarding, and loudly proclaim, every ten seconds, that "all's well in beautiful Mud City by the Bay."

"Mr. Adams, set the watch. And folks, if I were you, I would be fast asleep before your time for watch hits."

I grabbed our senior NCO, PN2 Suter, and simply told him to "set the watch." He quickly came up with a plan, and the rest of us leapt to the tents. The ground was hard and cold, and we were wet and stinking, but the wind was gone. Sleep was instantaneous for some, but unattainable for others. Our brains were on speed and could not easily slow down. If we did sleep for the twenty to thirty minutes before our watch, it was next to impossible to wake up again.

We were all being watched. ENS John Muggs and Rosy Rosenzweig had a tent to share. It was tight quarters, and they touched. Officer and enlisted. Where they touched, they could sense each other's warmth. It was only seconds before they were huddled tightly together. No words were spoken. Mutual survival was their common language. Rank and rate was immaterial. We all quickly did the same in each tent.

An air horn screamed after what seemed to be only a few minutes of blessed unconsciousness.

"Incoming!" screamed the instructors.

"We need to move the camp to the other side of the river, *quickly*. Grab your tents and move them across the mud river, now."

Out we stumbled, confused and disoriented, but the orders were clear. One by one, we pulled up the tents and poles and stakes and carried them to the muddy river. It was about thirty yards wide, and only an inch or two of water sparkled darkly on top of the stinking ooze. We all leapt into the abyss only to be swallowed by knee deep mud. Moving across the gap was next to impossible. Our boots sank deeper if we struggled. So finally, in desperation, while imaginary mortars dropped all around (per the voice on the bullhorn), we fell forward and tried to swim on top of the mud. This worked better, but our canvas tents began to absorb mud, and dragging them along was torture to already tired and aching muscles.

Progress was frustrating and slow. To cross approximately thirty yards of deep sticky mud, we would need to fall forward, drag the heavy canvas forward, pull our boots and legs out of the sucking muck, leap forward, and do it all again. Some tried to swim on their backs, and some tried to somersault, but the ooze won each time. The instructors remained loudly angry at our slow progress, but they were enjoying the thirty-minute break they had while watching our slow progress across this seemingly unending obstacle. The tents were coated with mud, and they stunk when each pair crawled out of their section of foul smelling primordial muck. We were reborn again on land. The tents were set up, and a watch was set once again. We leapt into the shelters, formed a human ball, and tried to sleep.

"All's well in beautiful Mud Haven by the Bay," sang out loudly again, by the changing men on watch, for about thirty minutes.

"Incoming!" again launched us into the stinky, muddy river Styx, and we clawed to the other side once again. The instructors really seemed to enjoy this. It took lots of time, and it was both cold and exhausting. Their stated goal for our time here was to overcome our natural tendency to avoid being wet and dirty. Simply stated, wet and dirty would be a favorite future operating environment, if we were to make it to the Teams. Future training events would seek out the darkest foulest environments for diving and patrolling. The enemy did not like this environment either, so if there was a clandestine way in, the dark and dirty way was often unguarded.

This time the tents stayed put for over an hour.

"Boat leaders, get your men up, and assemble by your tents for inspection," was passed calmly through the handheld megaphone. The instructor was standing by a large roaring fire made from beach wood and lumber imported for this event. He was warm and dry and *smiling* as we were about to be launched on a fabricated patrolling mission of his design. But first, it was time for the daily inspection.

One sailor and his tentmate had decided to quit. They could not sleep, and they planned together to walk away. Only the man on watch saw them leave. They walked to the fire and announced their decision. The bell on the back of a pickup truck rang three times, twice. No sleeping ears heard the noise, but one tent was now empty. An instructor then dragged the tent away.

We were standing in boat crew formations now, listening to our teeth chatter, and waiting for the daily medical inspection. I had been informed of the loss of two men and adjusted the count in my head. We were down to thirty-two men, just over half of what the class had started with. We were told to remove all our clothing, by the approaching corpsman. This was not fun.

"Stop shivering," ordered a seemingly serious instructor, as the corpsman began his examination looking for cuts or signs of infection. We were all still covered with mud where exposed skin was, but we were stark naked and standing at attention with only our helmets on, and wooden guns held properly at our sides. Pale, muscular, almost frozen bodies were lined up for the inspection. I was shivering so hard that I was afraid my teeth would crack. It had been a long, frigid time since our last warm meal.

I tried to smile at the instructor. I was sure that he was making an insanely cruel joke. It had been an incalculable time since I remembered not shivering. We all did not think about it much because thinking only led to doubts, and doubts could lead to fear. Fear could lead to failure, and failure was simply not acceptable.

"Goddamn it, that is an *order*. Stop shivering," he screamed, with his hot breath and spittle spattering in my face. He appeared quite angry, and focused like he wanted to teach me about some unknown knowledge of his own. He knew something that I did not know yet.

I realized, strangely and with alarm, that he thought this was possible. After a moment to digest this unfathomable demand, I decide to make every effort to at least appear to try to turn off the shivering. This reflex was an essential, and protective, automatic body response to cold. It seemed silly, of course, to accomplish this unreasonable command, but I knew he would need to see me try.

"Yes, Instructor," I replied as seriously as I could, knowing in my heart that this must be a game he was playing with my mind. After all, I was standing, naked as a jaybird, with a helmet on my head, and a wooden gun at my side, at attention.

With great physical effort and monk-like concentration, I gritted my sandy teeth, heard the grains crackle and crunch, slammed my eyes hard shut, took a deep cleansing breath, and flexed every quivering muscle in my body until I was rigid as a board. I was putting on a show for him.

The shivering stopped, to my great surprise. I was hypothermic, wet, and naked, and I now wanted the shivering to come back to warm me. But, sadly, it would not come back now, nor would it for a very long time. Tonight, I was going to miss the ability to shiver.

Buddhist monks can control their heart rate, blood pressure, and other autonomic functions. This is well documented. I had seemed to accomplish the same feat. I had no idea how. The instructor knew it could be done because he had done it himself in the past.

"Pain is just fear leaving the body," he would chuckle out loud at times.

The tormentor moved on, seemingly satisfied with my accomplishing the very unlikely. The corpsman continued down the line, inspecting for cuts or infections. We had been in the foul smelling, evil infused, mud flats for a long time now, and we made for a memorable group. Our corpsman snapped a picture of the formation, and it showed a line of gaunt, completely naked bodies standing at attention, with our helmets on, wooden guns at "order arms," and black mud obscuring our faces and hands where discarded clothing did not cover skin.

My innate, protective ability to shiver was lost. I would not regain that necessary defense against the cold for over a year. This made the cold even colder. The body would need to find other ways to generate heat. It might hold urine longer, and fight the desire to void. Conservation is automatic, but it would still allow me to fill my wet suit with warm urine on cold swims.

Inspection was over. No new serious cuts or infections were found. We all took our helmets off, lay our wooden, broomstick rifles on the wet ground, and scrambled into the filthy, wet uniforms we had removed. They were icy cold, and smelled like the sewage we were living in. Dragging wet clothing onto our now wind dried skin was just one more outrageously planned test or torture. The wet, muddy cloth would cling to our skin, and rake it with sand that felt like tiny ice crystals scraping our legs and arms. Our bodies would warm the wet cloth to a more acceptable temperature, but it would cost us stored calories in the process. This seriously sucked.

The night shift had arrived recently, but the sun was not yet set. It was darkening, and we were eating the instructor-provided C-rations again, sucking the sugar and powdered coffee from their containers, and squeezing every milligram of cheese or peanut butter from the packets. No hot meals would be provided in the mud flats. Most of us had not had a bowel movement in days, since we ate mostly carbohydrates and protein, and every calorie was being burned for fuel to survive the extreme chills and muscle demands.

The sun had set while we ate. We were interrupted, while eating, by an instructor, to have us all stand and "wave goodbye to Mr. Sun."

Evening meal was digesting, and we were called to the fire, one boat crew leader at a time. Boat Crew One went first.

"Now, sir, you have a mission to execute. Move your crew to the fire. You have ten minutes there to get your crew warm, while you and I work on the details of your mission."

I was suspicious of this offer of unexpected warmth. More likely, we would get close and then be ordered into the ocean again. We stood fast.

"Move it sir, your team only has nine minutes now," he growled with authority.

Oh well, I thought, *it is what it is, and I can't change it.* So I told the team to move to the inviting and roaring fire, and stay together. Sparks fluttered and swirled in the dark air above the logs. The smell of the wood fire was intoxicating. The instructor was moving easily towards the ambulance, and I followed, with reservations. He was dressed in green fatigue pants tucked into his jungle boots, with a blue and gold, double thick, T-shirt tucked tightly into his waist. The sleeves were rolled up slightly to make room for bulging biceps, and the stripe of yellow inner cloth glowed in the reflected light from the fire. The shirt was blue on the outside layer and had a yellow inner layer, which had become a casual uniform trademark of the current UDT/SEAL members. It was more often worn with khaki bathing shorts made famous in World War II, where frogmen wore their shorts, adorned with a green web belt. The belt supported a leather handled K-Bar knife with a MK-13 flare taped to its sheath.

I was waiting for an explosion, a gunshot, or an order to get wet, but nothing happened, and I watched the crew make it to the fire, and stand there steaming, as clouds of water vapor rolled off their wet clothes as if they were on fire. Quiet smiles appear in their reflected faces as heat attacked their wet clothes and skin. I wanted to be there with them.

"Fall seven times and stand up eight."
—Japanese proverb

Chapter 15
Wednesday early – Day 3

HOURS WITHOUT SLEEP - 56
5 OFFICERS AND 27 ENLISTED

It was now 0200, and we had not slept more than a few fitful minutes all week. We were all feeling a bit dingy. I was certainly no exception.

"OK sir, here is your mission. You are to patrol from the fire to the ocean, using the sand dunes for cover. Once you hit the hard-packed dirt beyond the dunes, turn south and patrol for thirty minutes. Do not pass into Mexico. There is a fence marking the border. Once you have patrolled thirty minutes, reverse course, and patrol back to this location using the dunes for cover. The fire will be visible."

"Oh, and by the way, we will be looking for you, and we have night vision goggles. Do not cross the fence into Mexico or get spotted by our roving vehicles. Clear?"

I repeated the plan, and acknowledged that I would carry out the mission. I wanted very much to join my team at the fire.

As soon as I arrived at the fire and my own clothes start to steam and dry, Rosy Rosensweig came up to me.

"Sir, I am not leaving this fire." Though he would not look me or the others in the eye, he sounded quote firm.

It was our jobs to start the dialog we had all used before.

"Don't do it." "Don't think about it." "We are all in this together; we need you."

Our different voices chimed in with similar messages, but we were not making much of an impression.

It seemed a cruel test to allow us to get warm after all this time being numb. Once again, the instructors seemed to have devised a diabolical test. It was clear that no amount of talking was going to change his mind, so I came up with a plan.

"Rosy, look, I have an idea. We don't leave here for a few minutes yet, and we need you to come with us."

"Not doing it, sir. I hate to let you down, but I think I am done now."

I could hear the new resolve, and the deep sadness, in his voice. He was glancing at us sideways, afraid to see what our reactions might be. The crew watched in tired disappointment. We all liked him.

"Think about this, Rosy. We are alone here, and the instructors are elsewhere. Go down the ridge to our tents where our gear is. Pull out your dry field jacket and put it on under your wet shirt. You will be warm. It is still dark, and they will never know."

We had given him both a glimmer of hope and a fighting chance to survive the biting air. He looked at me, and he looked at the fire, and the others whispered encouragingly for him to try. We were a team, we believed in each other, and we wanted him to stay with us. This was what he needed to reach deep inside, and be willing to face the extreme, indescribable ache of wintery cold again. We were his friends, and one day, we would likely be asked to put our lives on the line for each other.

Now, it was simply our goal to complete the next event.

The sense of *team* we had worked weeks to develop seemed irrelevant to Rosy at this time of individual survival, but quitting was a failure too, and we had sworn to each other that we would not allow failure if, as a team, we could help. We were offering him help. Save face now. Take one more step with us. He took it, and off to the tent he and his swim buddy slithered carefully, to execute this new plan for warmth.

"Guys, let's get ready to go as soon as they get back. The fire must not be allowed to tempt him again."

Rosy and his smiling swim buddy returned with Rosy looking a bit huskier. The dry thick jacket was now under his shirt, but he was smiling again. A few of us were jealous.

"Move out in single patrol file," I ordered. "Remember, we are being watched, so keep it slow and move quietly." We moved away from the fire immediately, on patrol, as directed.

Another idea began to form, as I moved the team off on our silly, time-gobbling mission. It seemed to me that they were just trying to keep us moving until dawn, when food and a new set of instructors would arrive. Like clockwork, new instructors arrived every eight hours, fresh and full of innovative ideas on how to test our resolve. So, after patrolling 300 yards along the muddy canals, half way to the ocean, wooden guns at the ready, I hesitated. As was mission typical, I was second in the patrol order, while the point man, MM3 Dave Banton, was setting the direction and speed of the patrol. The point man looked back when I paused. We were in a depression surrounded by small dunes, so I held up a single fist signaling stop. All six men stopped with me as directed, and I moved to our point man.

"Rally up, I have an idea," I passed to Dave. I waved my index finger in a circle over my head, and he followed me back, as we all gathered.

"This is all on me guys, but I don't think they can see us now, and the more we move, the more likely we are to be seen. Let's stay here in the dunes for thirty minutes, or more, and get some sleep. We will rotate sentry duty every five minutes, and Rosy you are first. If anyone sees an instructor coming, get us all up, and we will pretend to be returning from our patrol."

It seemed logical and dangerous at the same time, but no one wanted to argue at a chance for a few minutes' sleep, especially if the boom would likely fall on someone else if caught. And just like that, *poof*, there were sleeping bodies huddled together in the soft dune sands.

There had been some initial grumbling and whining about getting caught, but the lure of sleep, even a few minutes, had been too great to resist. Anyway, they could all say I ordered it, and the pain of punishment would be mostly mine – they *hoped*.

I could not sleep, as I lay flat and burrowed into the soft earth, looking for warmth that was not there. I was worried that I was making a mistake.

Mistakes were allowed it seemed, but failure was not. I could see the instructor's truck driving around. I suspected they were looking for us.

I would learn, as training went on, that other training classes had figured out this same ploy, and the instructors admired the deception. After all, we were training to do difficult missions, in places where we were not supposed to be, and where there were no rules. The men were already asleep, bundled, hugging tightly in pairs for warmth, as Rosy peeked up over the dune looking for the "enemy."

Here we were in the muddy, stinking slime of sewage and ocean brine, and I was the new class leader. There was no more hiding. My plan to hide had been rewritten by fate. I was not sure that I could convince the instructors that I had what they needed in a combat-capable officer. I was watching them, and they were watching me.

The other boat crews were scattered about making it harder for instructors to keep track of movements. The missions continued all night, and by dawn, four more men had called it quits. They were just suddenly gone.

> "When you get into a tight place and everything goes against you... never give up then, for that is just the place and time that the tide will turn."
> —Harriet Beecher Stowe

Chapter 16
Hump Day Wednesday – Day 3

HOURS WITHOUT SLEEP - 58
5 OFFICERS AND 23 ENLISTED

Dawn broke Wednesday with a cool orange sun peaking over the sandy dunes behind us. The instructors' shift change was still hours away, and we were huddled in another dune depression, opening our field C- rations for breakfast. Another two swim pairs had quit separately during the night. It seemed that in each case they had decided to quit together. To walk away from a swim buddy was much harder than doing it together. In both cases the instructors had tried to make sure the decisions were individual decisions to quit. Their attempts to prevent someone from being dragged to failure by another was brief but sincere. They accepted their decisions finally, and allowed them to be whisked away.

Frank had a Ham and Eggs, Chopped B-3 unit, which was much better than my Ham and Lima Beans B-2 unit. One had cheese spread, and the other had peanut butter, for the hard tack crackers that came with both. Dessert was either a palatable pound cake, or the less enjoyable fruit cake. Both were essential for survival. Unfortunately, both meals came in cans that needed to be opened with the tiny metal P-38 folding can openers provided. It was unfortunate, because we could barely feel our fingers. The so-called "John Wayne" device was difficult, and using it was downright painful.

There were matches for the three unwanted cigarettes also provided, and some proposed starting a fire with the paper boxes so we could warm our fingers. Frank freaked out at the suggestion, and vetoed it, for fear that it would bring unwanted attention from the currently absent instructors. So he sat in his spot of sand looking longingly at his can of food while sucking the cheese spread from the brown pouch that he had gnawed a hole in. He could not open his can of needed ham and eggs, but fear of doing something wrong and getting caught weighed heavily on him. This was his second attempt, and he would die trying if necessary. *Certainly, they would resuscitate me?* he thought from time to time.

His swim buddy reached over and carefully opened the can for him. Team.

Rosy was sucking the last of the Tabasco from the tiny red bottle provided and feeling quite at home, but he worried that his forbidden field jacket would be discovered now that the sun was coming up. If he took it off, he was sure he would freeze to death. If he left it on, he was sure he would be discovered, and he was wondering if the punishment would be worse than freezing to death. He was too numbed to make an intelligent decision, so he quietly pushed more peanut butter onto his cracker which he then sprinkled with the sugar and instant coffee provided. It tasted good, and he could feel the caloric warmth reaching out from his gut.

"Anyone have a Tabasco they don't want?" whispered Rosy.

"I'll trade you for your two Chicklets gum," came a voice next to him. A trade was made, and a few more minutes of silence passed peacefully. The instructors were tired too, and they were more than happy to stand by their fire and let us eat, while we contemplated the day ahead.

There was no published schedule of events that we could see, but stories of past weeks had given us some clues. Today was our half way point for the week, and if we could make it through today and tonight, rumor had it that we would make it all the way. Thursday or Friday was supposed to be a demolition day, to test our resolve under fire. That sounded like fun compared to the tasks so far.

"OK Studs. Breaks over. Bring your trash to the fire and drop it in," squawked the megaphone.

"Now, form up, by boat crew, for inspection and announcements. Mr. Adams, report your class."

This was not new. I was supposed to maintain an accurate count of remaining men. "Boat crews, report your count to me." I managed to order with authority.

After each boat crew reported in we huddled and counted.

"Sir, Class 81 is all present and accounted, twenty-eight men, Instructor." Interestingly, the other instructors were gathering as if something was going to happen. It made us nervous.

Instructor Steve Frisk stepped forward and received my salute. "Very well, sir," he responded.

"Radioman Third Class Thomas Valentine, front and center," came the next order.

Tom did not hear the order. He was cold and shivering.

His boat crew heard it and pushed him forward tentatively as they repeated the instruction to him.

Tom looked around confused and saw the instructors moving toward him. He came to attention and we all watched.

"Radioman Third Class Thomas Valentine…" Instructor Frisk pretended to read from a clipboard. "The Secretary of the Navy has reposed special trust and confidence in the patriotism, valor, fidelity and professional excellence of you this day. In view of these qualities and your demonstrated leadership potential and dedicated service to the United States Navy, you are therefore, promoted to Radioman Second Class."

It took a minute to sink in. This was not where these ceremonies usually occurred. He was sleep deprived and confused. So, he just stood there and grinned.

"Hooyah!" came our collective cries.

The instructors all came by and shook his hand. The corpsman came up with some white adhesive tape and rigged a second chevron under the single chevron currently on Tom's helmet.

Once all the congratulations were in order, it was necessary to honor him. With the encouragement of the instructors we gathered him up and carried him by all four extremities to the shallow mud puddle nearest us. With laughing, yelling, and Tom wriggling hardily, we slung him out into the mud. It was a good moment for all.

Tom climbed up the small embankment, muddy but smiling, looking for guidance on what was next.

"Next evolution is clam digging, and we want some clams for our lunch today."

"Boat crew leaders bring your boats to the canals. It is low tide now and the clams are ready for picking."

"Hanrath, get your newly refreshed, and warm, body over here, and find me some clams," ordered Instructor Tyvdik. He pointed to the waist-deep mud left behind by the receding tide.

"Let me see a perfect belly flop, Hanrath, and then feel under your body and find me some clams. Just keep feeling around until you find something hard."

Tom had been a superb competitive diver in school, and the instructors knew it.

Kerplop! went Tom in complete disregard to his great ability, and his body lay flat in the sucking, stinking tidal mud. After only a few seconds he pulled his right hand up, and in it was a small muddy clam.

Tyvdik smiled. "OK Gents, that is how it is done, so let's make a line to join him in the hunt."

"However, I need you each to enter the mud with a dive better than the one before."

"Turn your IBS upside down and use it as a spring board for your dive into the depths of this foul, fecal collection of putridness. And get us some clams for dinner."

One by one the line progressed to the inverted rubber diving board, and one by one, a flip or a spin would end with a loud sucking plop into the muck. Cheers followed, and these encouraged more dangerous acrobatics.

Then Randy came running down the line for his turn, remembering his stories of drunken aviators dive bombing tables in the officer clubs. He hit the IBS full force and launched his body forward in a perfect swan dive.

To the horror of all watching, Randy landed head first in the muddy crap, where only one inch of water trickled slowly towards the sea. The crunching noise as his head and shoulders buried themselves in the mud sounded like every bone in his neck must have collapsed on themselves. Everyone stood in shocked sudden awareness that something bad had just happened.

Nothing moved at first, and then his legs started frog kicking and twisting, and Instructor Tyvdik screamed to those nearby to save him. He could not breathe three feet deep in the muck, and he could not work himself free. No one said it, but some were wondering if Randy would ever walk again.

Two men nearest him, waded against the sucking slime, and worked to his legs sticking up. They pulled together, and slowly – *very slowly* – extricated his head from the muck. There was a collective silence until the tarry black head and shoulders emerged, and two bright white eyeballs showed through the black.

"Hooyah, Instructor," he yelped with zeal, and followed it with his famous laugh. His cackle let everyone know he would live to dive another day.

Dawn was full upon us now, but lunch was still hours away, and ENS Fields was once again being challenged by the instructors to do more. He was doing push-ups again, after a lackluster jump into the mud, that disappointed them. His swim buddy was encouraging him, and making sure the instructors knew he was trying to keep the teamwork alive. But somehow, it seemed his buddy was earning special attention. He stayed in a leaning rest position and watched.

"Faster, Mr. Fields, faster," screamed an instructor as he tried to count out the requested fifty push-ups. His arms were trembling from the effort, and he was spitting mud that was dripping down from his nose and forehead.

"Mr. Fields, did you just spit on my boots?" roared an incensed instructor.

"No sir, uh I mean no, *Instructor*," he replied remembering that the enlisted instructors did *not* like being called sir. Sir, was a term reserved for officers and the difference often quoted was that the enlisted men "worked for a living."

Two more instructors came over to watch the struggle. There had been prolonged discussions in the last few days, by all the shifts of instructors, as to whether Mr. Fields was going to graduate. The issue that kept coming up was, that there was something difficult to identify, that made the instructors uncomfortable about his leadership skills. He had done OK as a boat crew leader, but he was often seen having unnecessary discussions with his crew about what to do next. Lead, follow, or get out of the way. That was expected of a future SEAL. Indecision in combat was never acceptable. It was not always necessary to be right, but it was always necessary to decide.

The decision had been made the evening before, by the fire, that if Mr. Fields did not suddenly display a yet unseen, barrel full of leadership, then they would focus on running him out of training today. How they would do this was not clear, but in the past, when all the instructors piled on abuse for a sustained period, most men broke.

"Hit the water, Mr. Fields, and clean that filth off you."

"Hooyah, Instructor," came the weak, but willing, response. He ran to the ocean waves and walked into the icy Pacific. His swim buddy followed but was dropped to a leaning rest position again. The rest of the class nearby watched this happen with a quiet curiosity, since the rest of them were not being ordered to join him as usually happened. All three instructors followed him to the ocean edge as Mr. Fields began doing push-ups in the surf.

Usually, when a given task is failed, and the given response given is *I can't*, the instructors, who are waiting for that moment in all of us, attack with a vengeance. They scream and kick and push and prod the trainee with the intent of generating more adrenalin. With the adrenalin push and the fear of failure, the trainee is faced with a simple decision – do more or quit.

But this was not the case with ENS Fields, the training cadre's consensus was that he lacked something that would allow the instructors to support his goal to lead them as an officer. They would not allow this officer to graduate. He would do well elsewhere. There was no doubt about that, but he would not lead their teammates into combat.

The minutes of harsh, penetrating crashes of waves sapped the strength from his arms. The muddy, salty water streamed off his short-cropped hair. He was stuck in the leaning rest position. He could not do more, so he held fast as the instructors circled and demanded more.

"Are you *quitting* on us, Ensign?"

"No, Instructor," came his committed cry.

"It looks like you are quitting."

"Give me fifty more push-ups, now," barked another instructor.

"Yes, Instructor" came the response drowned out by the one-foot crunching waves. He dropped down into the froth, and tried to push up one more time. It was impossible. He could not feel his hands or feet. He was shivering uncontrollably, but he was not going to quit. Surely, they would stop this soon.

A brief huddle of instructors gathered to discuss their plan. Mr. Fields was tough, and it was showing, but a decision had been made.

"Out of the water, Mr. Fields. You have failed to accomplish the required task, so we must assume you have quit."

There was a quiet sadness to the announcement, and most of us did not hear it.

"I am *not* quitting," squeaked an uncertain ENS Vernon Fields.

Yet suddenly he was gone. A truck door opened, and he got in it. We were stunned. One more officer was gone. No explanation was given.

When next we made it back to the training compound, we would find his helmet with his name and white stripe on it, lined up next to the others that had quit. But to this day, I do not believe he quit, and I hope his career in the Navy took him to wonderful places. At the same time, I am sure the instructors made the right decision. It is very hard to describe, but there is a very identifiable look and persona that men recognize in leaders. Vernon did not have it.

"Never confuse a single defeat with a final defeat."
—F. Scott Fitzgerald

Chapter 17
Wednesday – Night comes again – Day 3

HOURS WITHOUT SLEEP - 70
4 OFFICERS AND 19 ENLISTED

"Boat crews, man your boats. Mission briefing in five minutes. Boat crew leaders, at the fire in five."

While the instructors gathered to inform us of the next mission, Instructor Crawford wandered our way, and spit a large slick odiferous wad in one crew's direction. He chewed Red Man tobacco on these night missions to keep him awake and aware.

The seven men of Boat Crew Two waited, wet, and shivering.

"Line up men. I have a night time treat for you," he announced, as he produced his rolled-up bag of chew. Then one by one he walked down the line ordering each man to enjoy a chew with him. Into each mouth was delivered a sweet smelling, but burning, load of fresh moist tobacco.

"Chew it. Don't swallow it," he advised, as he walked down the line of apprehensive recipients of his questionable largess.

"And no spitting until I tell you too."

Then he came up to ENS Albracht, and offered the last plug of chew. He reached forward as strands of dark black tobacco snaked out from his hand and Randy almost retched at the smell. He thought quickly, and stated firmly,

"No thank you, Instructor, I need to set a good example for my men here. No tobacco touches these lips." He smiled his typical silly smile, and waited, while the nasty sweetish smelling glob was waved at him.

The ploy worked, as it caught the instructor off guard. He knew well that soon there would be some coughing and possible puking noises, coming from the line of men behind him. He also remembered that officers would be required to perform every task alongside their men. What caused him to pause and think, was that they had also told each officer that they would be evaluated for leadership, and any doubt in this area would be met with the worst possible outcome.

"Well sir, I guess I will let you have another chance later to take me up on my kind offer," he slurred, as he spit again, and turned away.

"OK, Boat Crew Two, you may all spit now."

Immediately the entire crew simultaneously spit their wads at the mud and wiped the dark burning liquid from their chins. Except for PN2 Suter who spit, but continued to chew, seemingly enjoying the nicotine rush. He still missed his Marlboros. One man promptly wretched and dry heaved. Their heads buzzed, and their hearts raced even faster. ENS Albracht turned away and smiled in relief.

"Alright men, it's Tuesday night, and we have a long week ahead. Later tonight, we are going to race back to Coronado, and you better be there by midnight, or you will miss midnight rations at the mess hall. But first I need a song."

Wait? Did he say Tuesday? We all thought it was Wednesday. *Crap, that can't be true.* We looked at each other and fatigue got in the way. *What day was this? Could we really have that far to go? How many sunrises have we seen?*

It was Wednesday, but one more mind game was playing with our senses. Core body temperatures had been dropping in all of us, and thinking was more difficult. Sleep was a distant memory, and our heart rates had sped up to a resting rate above 100. We were on sleepless, speed mode. Some things we thought we saw were just optical illusions now.

What day is this again? No one was completely sure, except the instructors.

The sun had set on what we were, by consensus, agreeing was Wednesday. Randy had been chosen to lead us in the requested song, and he was leading us in a rousing chorus of "Ole Dan Tucker", a song from the Civil War days that he had learned in his youth in Iowa, and was teaching us all to sing.

"Now ole Dan Tucker was a fine old man
Washed his face in a frying pan
Combed his hair with a wagon wheel
Died with a toothache in his heel

Get out of the way, old Dan Tucker
You're too late to get your supper
Get out of the way, old Dan Tucker
You're too late to get your supper"

We all stood in a circle, barely erect, as Randy danced a jig and instructed us in the tune and words. We tried to remember the words. We were awful, and the instructors were enjoying it. At least one person seemed sound asleep in a standing position. The shift would change soon. We had consumed our dinner C-rations and had endured one last inspection, stark naked, by our ever-watchful corpsmen. They did not want to lose a trainee to skin cellulitis, a preventable infection made more likely by the filthy abuse we were exposing our bodies to.

The early evening wore on with more social events designed to keep us awake. Sleep deprivation was taking a toll, and we were entertaining the instructors. But the fun was soon to end.

The new instructor cadre arrived as we continued to entertain all with stories and songs, made up by each person able to do so. It was time to go back to Coronado. We knew this since the tents had been packed, and the trash had been policed up. Even the instructors' fire was out, and ashes were checked and rechecked.

"Good evening, Gents," crooned the new cadre leader. "I am pleased to report that three more men quit so far today. They are warm and comfortable in their beds now. They had hot steaming showers, and they will have yummy steak and eggs for breakfast this morning. Do any of you want to join them in their pleasure?"

"Hell no, Instructor!" I whooped, and the whole gang joined in.

"Hell no, Instructor!"

"Well that is fine with us. But your next event is dangerous, and I need you all to pay close attention to the safely brief."

We gathered as a group in front of the speaker and *tried* to focus on what he said or meant. Focus was difficult. We were not much better than walking zombies now. Earlier, they had marched us around the camp, and when ordered to march towards a large van, we found ourselves marking time, as we plowed, in rows, into the side of the van. It seemed odd, but it also seemed appropriate, to just march there as a group, counting cadence, and going nowhere. It was certainly better than doing push-ups in the surf zone.

"You will be taking your boats back to Coronado tonight. You will not be allowed to leave the water. There are waves and swells tonight that you will navigate through going out and coming in. You will likely be disoriented by the darkness and lights around you. There will be no safety boats out tonight, so you must remain in sight of land at all times. We will have a truck following you along the beach, and if you need it, for an emergency only, you may paddle ashore and present to the corpsman."

"The paddle will take several hours, as you recall from your daytime trip, to get here. There is one less boat now. You have lost some more classmates. Your new crews need to work together, and remember as always, it is good to finish first. So just to ensure you are all awake, drop your paddles next to the boats and hit the surf. Keep your swim buddy with you. By the way, only one boat crew still has the original seven men. You all might want to learn from the mighty dwarfs."

"Hooyah!" we replied together, and once again made our way across the beach to the gently moving Pacific waters. Cold did not matter much now. Frigid was all we knew. The water hitting our already almost numb legs did not sting much anymore. We were walking snowmen. It was Wednesday night, and the demolition day would come with sunrise. There was a perceived end-point now. Survive was the order of the day.

"Up boats. Forward march."

And all four remaining boat crews marched into the surf, carrying their IBS by the side handles, thinking of how to win the miles-long race home. Thinking was difficult.

A whistle sounded, and without hesitation, all four boat crews dropped to the ground, let the surf pass over them, and covered their heads, as the boats splashed down next to them.

Two long tweets followed, and the boat crews attempted to turn around their boats while crawling towards the sound. This had been happening more frequently now. We were responding, like Pavlov's dogs, to whistle commands. One whistle, drop and cover. Two whistles, and we low-crawled to the sound. Three whistles meant recover and stand fast. We were practicing every day for "So Solly Day," when demolition blasts would surround us all, and our need to follow these commands could be life and death events.

The four remaining crews were redirected and launched without trouble. The waves were less than two feet high. The moon was only a sliver and gave off a dim light. The stars were out like snowflakes. We began our slow transit back to the training area, but as we gathered outside of the instructors' glares, we agreed that going slow made the most sense. Whatever waited for us in Coronado was certainly worse than a gentle paddle on a quiet starlit sea.

Unseen by three of the boat crews, one sailor remained ashore, and his swim buddy had a new partner. He had let the thoughts of warmth invade his brain, and his now muddled thoughts could not focus on why he was there. He needed the cold to stop. He had other options in life. There were other options out there for him. *Besides*, he thought, *this whole thing is just stupid.*

He watched the others paddle away and tried to smile, but there was no time. The instructor was literally pushing him up the beach to the waiting truck that would transport him back to a normal place. He felt both relief and personal shame, but he knew he would get over it. There was a great big warm navy out there for him.

"Sea monsters!" screeched a sailor as he beat the water, with his paddle, in fear. His screaming could be heard by all. They had been at sea now for over an hour.

"Calm him down," whispered ENS Johnson, the coxswain. "Pull him into the boat." He was trying to scramble over the other side to get away from the seemingly real, and frightening, hallucination he believed was attacking us all.

ENS Muggs's boat had a paddler seeing an aircraft carrier bearing down on them at full speed. He had jumped overboard, and was swimming away. They had picked him out of the water, and he was confused as to where the carrier had gone. The snappy polar water had helped some. ENS Muggs was a bit shaken by this and decided to paddle his crew to the truck visible on the beach. As the boat approached, the corpsman came out with a light to signal them to him. As the boat approached, another crewman started yelling "Tidal wave! Tidal wave!" as he jumped overboard, to swim and wade ashore, in panic mode.

The corpsman had seen this *many* times before. He would calm the man down and get a report from the officer in charge. He would then brief the crew on sleep deprivation, and these common associated hallucinations. They still had at least an hour of paddling ahead, and they appeared to be keeping up with the main group, so the corpsman fed each member a half snickers bar, and allowed them to pass around his cup of hot coffee, which he refilled once, from his truck thermos. ENS Muggs was now their hero. "Good call, sir," muttered both Mike Suter and Rosy Rosenzweig.

"Off you go boys. No more sea monsters ahead, I promise." He chuckled as he helped push the boat out to sea again. He was a Team corpsman, and he loved his job. Where else could he have this kind of responsibility, and hopefully help train his future teammates?

The boat moved off into the dark froth of the rolling Pacific Ocean again. The dark was a friend. They felt exhausted all the time now, but were free from attack and harassment.

On shore however, was a blacked-out truck following their movements, and quietly discussing the state of the men that had just launched back to continue their mission.

"I think at least one will quit soon. They are operating on reserves now," Instructor Tyvdik noted.

"I don't know. These guys have taken everything we have thrown at them so far. Tonight, is the turning point. If they make it to sunrise they are likely to make it all the way. I hope they do, but let's have a test waiting when they come in," sighed an instructor. He thought of the respect these men had earned so far, and the responsibility he also shouldered for his teammates.

One boat was ashore already, but it was unnoticed by the other boats now spread out along the planned route. It was quiet at sea, except for the splash of paddles, and the next boat was nearing the end, far out from the shore.

"OK," whispered ENS Muggs hoarsely. "Let's make it towards the surf zone and the BUD/S area, guys. But paddle slowly and conserve energy. I don't see anyone there yet so we might be first. Maybe we can get a rest break. Pull together slowly."

Rosensweig, in the middle starboard position, was paddling slowly and sound asleep. His arms moved in rhythm, but he was feeling the warmth of home and the sting of a hot cheese burrito just off the stove. The smell was wonderful, and the heat and sustenance was causing a rush of pleasure in his gut. His whole body felt the warmth roll down to his legs. He was happy.

Then a splash from the paddler in front landed on his face, and he awoke. He wanted to go back to the warm, and he was not sure where he was. As consciousness slowly returned, he realized he was peeing in his pants again. It felt warm, so he just finished the task. Since his leg was bent to 90 degrees to paddle, he sadly realized that the new warmth would not make it to his boots where his toes begged for warmth. He could still taste the burrito.

"Muggs, you asshole! Can you please keep us straight?" came a voice from the front of the boat. There was no sense of officer/enlisted protocol now. This was survival mode, and all were equal. ENS Muggs was falling asleep, and the IBS would swerve slightly right or left as his paddle in the water moved. To the paddlers, this was unacceptable. Even the slightest misadventure, leading to wasted energy, was unforgivable now.

"I'm fine," he whispered, feeling guilty that he was steering from the more comfortable rear seventh man position while they paddled. The boat moved slowly towards the now visible white breakers just off shore from the training compound. There were no instructors in sight and no sign of the other boat crews. Either they were winning this event, or they were way behind.

"Ones out, twos out, threes out," whispered ENS Muggs, and two by two, the paddlers piled out of the boat into shallow water. It was calm and clear, and no one seemed around. Everyone took a quiet breath of relief.

Three minutes passed while they sat resting on the IBS that they had moved up to the dry sand, and without warning lights came over the high dunes in front of them.

"Drop, *you stinking maggots*. Feet on the boat. Leaning rest position," came the orders from a bullhorn.

One by one the seven men assumed the leaning rest position with feet elevated onto the IBS. They waited.

"Jesus Christ, Gentlemen, you are in *second* place. The winning crew is drinking hot coffee and resting. You first failures need to show us if you want to be here."

"Mr. Muggs, lead your crew in push-ups, now. Count them out. You will keep doing them until I get tired," smiled the instructor behind the light. More instructor shadows moved in the near distance.

"One, two, three...."

...thirty-one, thirty-two," he called as the count progressed. Frank Winget was starting to falter. His push-ups were barely moving up and down. Everyone was trying to conserve energy when none was left.

"Wing Nut, you skinny faggot, fall out for corrective instruction," yipped an instructor in the back. He had also been Winget's instructor only eighteen months ago, and had seen him quit in Hell Week with his old class (Class 72). If he wanted to make it this time, he would have to prove himself worthy of this second try.

"Hit the surf, and roll your sugar cookie, lazy ass up here to me, now."

Frank looked up and knew he was in for another test. He rolled off the IBS and groaned as he pulled himself up and waddled, in pain, to the penetrating winter ocean. He waded quickly into the surf zone, feeling the icy chill push blood from his feet towards his torso, and when he was thigh deep, he splashed noisily into the froth.

"Hooyah!" he whooped as he tried to run back to the beach. It was all about show now, and he knew that he was in the spotlight. He made it to the dry sand ten yards in front of his waiting tormentor, and dove into the softness. He rolled over and over, until his face, hands and clothing were completely stuck with the beach sand and smell. He pulled himself up and noticed that the boat crew was still in the leaning rest position watching.

"Drop, you lazy excuse for sea scum. Give me fifty four-count flutter kicks and then fifty push-ups right now."

Frank hit the sand again, and counted out the fifty four-count flutter kicks. Then he started to count out the required fifty more push-ups, but the numbed and incredibly tired arm muscles would not produce. He had been paddling for hours in an icy environment, and now he was back from an electrified dip in the hawkish waters behind him. All his track training could not measure up to the strain his muscles felt now. At push-up number eleven, he found himself unable to push off the ground. He grunted, and tried, and failed.

It was as if the instructor knew he would fail.

"We have a quitter here," he howled to the nearby group of instructors, and suddenly shadows became men, and the men were not happy.

One instructor walked up and kicked sand in his face, and spit on him. Another began to taunt him, about being a quitter. The third one materialized with a paddle, and began to shovel more beach onto his back. ENS Muggs and his crew could do nothing except witness.

"Fifty push-ups *now*, Winget, and I mean *right now*," squawked his first challenger.

"Twelve, thirteen..." he counted out as he pushed his body to respond.

"Bullshit, asshole. You start again at one."

He reached *deep* inside and began again. But after only seven more push-ups his muscles started to tremor and shake. He knew this feeling from his track days, when he had been pushed to his physical limit, and the stored energy was gone, and he could not run any faster. He was at the end of his rope. But he also knew that, somehow, he needed to continue, or his second Hell Week attempt would end in failure.

The instructors saw what they were looking for. Frank was at his physical end. His body would not allow him to go on. He was at the "line" that they had all seen before. Frank would have to step over the line and do what all his past life experiences had taught him was impossible, or he would have to quit.

"Start again. Give us fifty," yipped the circling hyenas, and they spit and kicked and slapped him. Adrenalin surged, and Frank began to move again. He began pushing out one dip after another, and each one surprised him. Each one brought him closer to total exhaustion and collapse. He would go until he collapsed, or his triceps exploded, but he would not stop trying.

He would not quit. The ignominy that he carried with him would not be allowed another chance at his future.

One slow push-up at a time, he dipped his chest to the ground and pushed back up. He lost count in his mind, but continued to count out loud. He was in a place he had never been before. His body was doing what he needed it to do, but he was unsure how it was happening.

"Fifty." He heard himself grunt. Sweat was dripping off his red, stinging, sandy nose, and he could not remember how he got there. He was as surprised as his watching boat crew that he had done it. He had accomplished the task, and done the impossible.

"So, you think it is all over now? You passed the test? Well you did not. Get your ass back in the ocean, and roll yourself back to me because we are going to do this until the sun comes up. Move it, you weak, inadequate, *shitbird*."

Incredulously, Frank moved back to the ocean as he contemplated doing this again and again until the sun came up. He did not know how many hours were left until sunrise, but something had changed inside him. He could feel it. He had stepped over the line of impossible.

Something had snapped in his brain, and he felt a warmth that he was unfamiliar with. He knew that he would go on. He knew that he had control over his muscles. Mind over matter now was real. He was not going to quit, and he was not going to fail. Not this time.

The instructors saw it too. They had all seen it many times before. Frank had been taken to his physical limit, and then he had stepped *beyond* that point. They could see it in his walk, standing a little taller. They could see it in his eyes, as he looked back at them with conviction and defiance. This was *exactly* what they wanted to see in every swinging dick they trained.

– *I am here. I am not going away. Do what you will* –

It was in his eyes, and his posture.

Still, just to make sure, they left him with his challenger, and moved away to the others in his boat crew. And Frank's challenge was made harder.

"Drop and give me one hundred push-ups," growled the instructor, but there was a different tone to the order. It had a hint of respect in it because he knew that Frank would complete the task now.

So did Frank.

"I'm playing; I'm here.
I'm going to fight until they tell me they don't want me anymore."
—Steve Nash

Chapter 18
"So Solly" Thursday Day 4

HOURS WITHOUT SLEEP - 86
4 OFFICERS AND 13 ENLISTED

Thursday's dawn came very slowly. There were still three boat crews, but two crews had only five men left. The night's activities had taken its toll. Clouds hid the light, and the wind was biting once again. Everyone was in pure survival mode. Feet were swollen and walking was excruciating. Toenails had fallen off or were hanging on by a thread. Numb hands and feet were a blessing now.

The whistle sounded, and all three boat crews hit the sand with open mouths, and hands on their green helmets. The paint was gone now from the top of everyone's helmet due to the rubbing of their heavy IBS.

Two more tweets, and the boats began to move like caterpillars with arms and legs towards the sound. Three final tweets, and the boats slowly rose under their groups of beaten and spent men.

Breakfast had been in the mess hall almost two miles away, and the food was hot and necessary once again. The room had been warm, and they had been allowed an entire thirty minutes to eat and use the facilities. It was impossible to do more than walk now. The swollen feet, sore heads and necks, and bent backs had been abused while carrying the heavy rubber boats.

However, one corpsman had made a mistake; he had pushed the boats to a run pace for the mile and a half back. There was shrill screaming and cussing heard most of the way, as the pace remained way too fast for the state of health we all suffered from. Most of the officers and senior enlisted begged to slow the pace, but common sense was lost, and the forced prisoner run continued. By the time we made it back, most of us were seriously pissed, and in pain beyond even our own imaginations.

Unfortunately for the corpsman who had overstepped his authority, Chief Petty Officer Wade Puckett was waiting for us to return. Corpsmen were not instructors. They were part of the support effort, but in some cases like this, they would be put in charge of a simple personnel movement. When Puckett saw what had happened and heard the moans of *his* class, he launched himself at the surprised corpsman.

He ordered us all to drop boats and take seats as he dragged the protesting miscreant around to the other side of a large metal CONEX (Container Express) box. We could hear him yelling as he banged his new enemy up against the CONEX box again and again.

Wade Puckett had been an assassin in Vietnam. He operated there independently and made bad people disappear. He had a high price on his head, offered by the Vietcong. But now, he was our class proctor and protector. He was our friend and advocate. He made sure we were given what we needed to succeed. Success, of course, was up to each individual, but the class had a mission to help each other, and he had a mission to see as many as possible make the cut.

The boats were stowed on the back of a six-by truck, slowly under our proctor's now very watchful eye. Two men had puked up breakfast on the run back, and he was feeding them Snickers and hot chocolate, produced willingly by the now contrite and clearly corrected corpsman.

We walked in slow formation, slow route-step, over the berm and past the O-course to the demolition area. Once there, our boats were recovered from the truck driven by the refocused corpsman, who kept watching Puckett out of the corner of his eye, fearing somewhat for his life.

Today was an important day for all. The logistics were extensive. There were numerous pre-staged small explosive charges placed – and gently marked – all over the sand dunes and ice plant areas. There was also a deep pit filled with water, an upright telephone pole set on either side; two trucks, each parked a short distance from a pole facing away from the pit. Suspended across the pit were two thick ropes about fifty feet long. There was an upper rope and lower rope set vertically apart by about six or seven feet. The upper rope was attached to the telephone pole on one side of the pit and strung through a pulley set on the telephone pole on the other side with its *free* end secured to the bumper of the truck parked there. The lower rope was similarly rigged to run to the second truck parked on the other side of the pit.

At that point, our brains were so deprived the set up looked impossibly elaborate. No time to think about it. We would discover it's function soon enough.

Up until now, I had succeeded in avoiding unnecessary extra attention. I had stayed as hidden and average as I could except when I absolutely *could not* – as class leader, following orders. Something was changing today as I looked at what was ahead. There were going to be loud explosions and perhaps guns firing around us. They were looking for fear. We did not think they would find any in the survivors of our class that were left. If fear was possible, we would have seen it already.

Additionally, I was starting to realize that our much smaller group was most likely to finish intact. There were only four officers left of the eight that started. I began to think about the day ahead.

The scream of a whistle, and we all hit the deck. Two more and we crawled as a group to the sound. This time instructors circled our group and pushed us closer together. Something was going to happen. We could feel it in the air.

Blam! The sky boomed around us, and the sand under us leapt up and threw us all six inches in the air. A dark cloud appeared on both sides of us, and sand began to fall from the sky.

"So Solly!" whooped the instructors in unison, as their private joke – saying "So Sorry" with a Vietnamese accent – was repeated once more. So Solly Day was here.

We all felt an elation we had not felt before. This was a combat environment. I loved the noises, and I loved the smells. I looked around and noted that most everyone seemed fine, but apprehensive. *Boom, blam, boom*, went three more close order explosions, and more sand and grey powder came out of the sky.

Three tweets, and we were on our feet again looking at the deep holes *very* close to where we were gathered. The tweets continued, and we were maneuvered to a new area covered with obstacles. John Muggs found himself next to a half-buried tire, level with his head.

Instructor Crawford came up to him with a yellow rectangle of half-pound TNT in his hand, and a time fuse sticking out of the top. He made sure John saw what it was, and then he placed it in the tire, one foot from his head. He lit the fuse and backed away with fingers in his ears. The fuse had about six inches to burn, which gave John about twenty seconds to decide what to do.

He decided to do nothing. Logic told him that Instructor Crawford must know something he did not. He would not be allowed to kill him, of that he was sure. Perhaps this TNT, which had no metal casing, would blow upwards or over him. He did not yet know about blast waves, but he was sure the instructor did. So, he deliberately put his fingers in his ears, closed his eyes, blew out half a lung of air, opened his mouth as he had been trained, and held his breath. The uncovered open mouth prevented a blast wave from doing instant damage to the lungs, ears, and sinus cavities, we were told.

The fuse burned down to the TNT block and fizzled out. It had been a fake designed to test him. He had passed without even wetting his pants.

No one else had been witness to John's individual test, since chaos reigned everywhere now. I felt invigorated by the confusion of activity. When the next whistle set sounded, I leaped to my feet and rushed ahead in order to be the first one there. It took some extra effort in the soft grit that I did not need to expend, but there was a new energy pulsing through me that I could not deny. The instructor with the whistle noticed, and I caught a hint of a smile. I could almost hear him thinking, *OK Mr. Class Leader, seems you are ready to accept the role. It's about time.*

That was when I knew I was going to finish. We all were. It was a new kind of adrenalin rush, and I liked it. I was going to let them *see* me now and learn more about me than I had planned before. I was still unsure about men like Chief Rogers – men with recent Team combat experience – accepting any of us, but I certainly wanted them to know that I was willing to try.

I decided to be first to everything that day, and I was. My classmates noticed too, and they liked it. It gave them energy to see that I still had something in reserve. No one balked at the demolitions all around us. No one freaked out or even expressed concern. We were going to make it together. This was our final team. There were seventeen of us left, and we liked what we saw.

It was nearing lunchtime, and we were gathered around the deep pit filled with oily black water and the ropes strung across it between telephone poles. The game we were being instructed in *seemed* simple. We were to hold onto the top rope, use the bottom rope for our feet, and walk across the pit without falling in. Doable. But the trucks at one end had the bitter ends of the ropes tied to their bumpers. There was something very suspicious about *that*.

There was a bit of a carnival atmosphere about this event. The man on the flying trapeze? So, one at a time, we tried to cross on the rope, and one at a time the trucks would back up and jump forward, throwing even the most determined man into the muck below. Glacial anguish and dirt had been our constant companions, so this additional insult was no shock. We cheered each try and laughed at each failure.

The instructors knew the statistics better than any of us, and they knew that, despite the grueling night planned, we would all finish. Today was a time to avoid injury.

One by one, we stepped onto the bottom rope, grabbed hold of the upper rope above our heads, and tried to inch across before we were thrown off. One by one, we failed. Then Hanrath started, and as soon as his now half-starved 130-pound body was on the lower rope one of the trucks backed up and the top rope went slack. So, he used his acrobatic diver training and flopped himself onto the top rope in a low crawl position. His hands pulled himself forward while his feet held tight behind him. He scrambled forward quickly like he was sliding down the rope Slide-for-Life obstacle, and was half way across before the instructors saw what he was doing.

We all started cheering for our first man to make it this far. The truck leapt forward and the upper rope he was now part of snapped upwards. He was flung up with it but his hands and feet wrapped tighter, and as soon as the rope was taut, he slithered farther along. The instructors were calling out orders to the truck driver in distress. "Back, jerk, up, slow, fast" were all suggestions as the cheering and laughing got louder. Tom, our acrobatic diver, was well past the half way mark.

The rest of us were sitting, as ordered, in the black smelly ooze of the pit, and enjoying this immensely. There were still explosions going off around us, spraying hot, filth-tinged water all over, as instructors threw loud explosive artillery simulators into the pit near the middle, but not directly under Tom.

Tom was smiling and anticipating success as his lithe body slipped further along. The instructors were admiring his innovation, but refusing to consider his success. The truck began to back slowly backwards until both ropes were in the pit. Tom was holding on and swimming forward now. The end and success was in sight. Then, unexpectedly, the truck surged forward, and Tom was flung rapidly toward the sky. As he left the stinky pit water, on his flight up, his feet came loose. The rope went taught, the G-forces on his body exceeded the expected, and his hands were torn loose as he catapulted into the air. On his way down, he twisted and reached for the rope one last time but it was out of reach, so he did what he was trained to do, and did a quick jackknife maneuver before splashing gracefully into the pit.

Instructors and tadpoles alike erupted into joyous applause as Tom emerged, black-faced from the sticky, floating slime, and explosive residue, with a white toothed smile, that all could see and enjoy. His past diving training had come in handy.

Lunch arrived as box lunches again, and it found us all waist deep in foul chemical laden water that smelled of burnt explosives. As we tried to eat from our boxes, the instructors kept blowing up charges in the water and beach residue around us. The sandwiches, hardboiled eggs, sugar packets, lettuce and mayonnaise, got eaten quickly, and so did a fair amount of foreign matter and foul chemical laden water. Yum.

The end was nearing, and we all knew it.

The rest of the day progressed just like every other day, but there was a new slowness to the events. There were seventeen men left under three boats. The boats seemed heavier, and movement was laborious.

The instructors were ensuring movement without further risk of injury. Running was not possible or requested. At dinner that evening, we were once again transiting the long walk to the mess hall, but running was now impossible. Feet and leg muscles were in such a state of pain and dysfunction that just walking was a monumental effort. Each footfall hurt from the swollen sole, up the bones, to the brain, which tried to ignore the insult again and again.

"Forward march," ordered the instructor as we moved towards a wall on the back side of the mess hall. All three boat crews moved unthinkingly towards the brick obstacle ahead. One by one, each crew reached the wall and was stopped by the immovable object in their path. But no one ordered halt, so we just pushed on against the barrier marching silently in place. The instructors seemed to enjoy our predicament, but interestingly none of us seemed to care. By now everything was running on automatic and "ours is not to reason why, ours is but to do or die." That was my thought as I imagined what soldiers must have done in Tennyson's "Charge of the Light Brigade". *Everyone knew that someone had blundered, but into the valley of death rode the six hundred...* was how I remembered it then.

> "Theirs not to make reply,
> Theirs not to reason why,
> Theirs but to do and die:
> Into the Valley of Death
> Rode the six hundred."

One step at a time, one event at a time, was the order of the day. We were finally directed to stop, and we rerouted inside to the waiting evening meal.

Each boat crew stayed together in a fog of exhaustion. Tempers flared; emotions were on the surface. Sometimes there was anger, sometime unexpected tears, and laughter at the oddest things. Emotions were difficult to manage. Each minute was just another minute closer to a finish that we did not allow ourselves to think about. There was a certain odd feeling that we all shared now. It was a mixture of feeling drunk and numb at the same time.

The mind still played tricks, by letting us see and hear things that were not there, but it was manageable, and pain was such a constant companion now it was simply part of us.

Sometimes we would hear musical instruments, or birds singing, and ask others if they heard it. Usually they did not, but medical studies have demonstrated that two factors were at play now. One is that pain receptors gratefully down regulate the pain signals when the pain is constant. The other phenomenon is that interaction with others experiencing pain can lessen the effect. The social supports we promised each other, and which we tried hard to enact, helped reduce the pain levels.

Into the Valley of Death, we rode... *together.*

"Failure is often that early morning hour of darkness which precedes the dawning of the day of success."
—Leigh Mitchell Hodges

Chapter 19
Secure Early – Friday Day 5

HOURS WITHOUT SLEEP - 110
4 OFFICERS AND 13 ENLISTED

Midrats (midnight rations), our blessed late-night meal, was witnessed by the mess hall stewards who thought they were watching the walking dead. There was still one long and difficult event left, but none of us knew this. The end was always kept a surprise, and there was usually a quiet but emotional announcement at the end.

Our boat crew had won almost all the competitions from day one. We still had seven men. The other two remaining crews were down to five each. Someone was keeping score, but we knew we were winning because we had been granted more than a few rest moments as winners. The intent of constant competition seemed to encourage maximum effort. Maximum effort would lead to total exhaustion sooner rather than later. Total exhaustion was one of the planned goals. Every man needed to find what he thought was his physical limit, and then he needed to be challenged to step past that point – *way* past it.

Because we were the first ones back in many events, we were also able to get to our vitamin and supplement stash more often than the others. It seemed to help, or we thought it did, and that made a difference. Even with a few minutes here and there, some vitamins, and a slick bottomed boat, we were suffering. We were anemic (as next week's blood tests would show when we tried to donate blood as a class), our feet were stuck, swollen in our boots, toenails had sloughed off, and our minds were still playing tricks on us.

It was past midnight. We had eaten our midrats and completed another boat and water event designed to keep us moving and busy so we would not think about another cutting, penetrating long night ahead. The instructors had been promising something special to the winners, and we thought about a nap or a piece of hot pizza, as we placed our boat back on our heads and moved to the truck where a corpsman and instructors waited.

There were three boat crews. It was time to start an event called Around the World. Each boat crew was taken to a different starting point, somewhere on the silver strand, between the hotels and the dunes south of the BUD/S area. Each team would walk a different course looking for clues until sunrise.

"Down boats," was ordered, and our crew dropped it like a lead weight. We were on the beach just behind the BUD/S area barracks. There were seven of us. It seemed that no one knew what to do next, so we stood quietly. The first phase officer LT Lyons was there, and this was unusual for this time of the very dark early morning. He came forward, and we snapped to attention.

"Hit the surf, and form a chain in the shallows, Gentlemen. It's time for some more surf appreciation." We moved together once again to the froth of breaking waves, turned towards our antagonist, linked arms, and sat down. The waves crashed over our shoulders, and the cold seawater moved like icy fingers into our boots, and agonizingly up our legs to our testicles, now drawn protectively up into our groins. We had long ago lost track of how many times we had done this same evolution.

This was a sensation that you just did not ever get used to. Our clothing sucked close to the skin, pushed by the weight of the water, and then the water had to find its way slowly between cloth and skin. Usually it was just better to dive in and let it all happen at once. Once the wet was caught between skin and cloth it began to warm. The heat from our bodies got sucked by osmosis into the water layer we now stored. It was a bit like a wet suit that traps water and warms it, but in this case, every wave caused movement, and every movement caused the slightly warmer water to rush away, and be replaced by more of Neptune's salty, heat-stealing habitat.

We were miserable once again. Then the three instructors walked into the surf with us.

"Boat crew number one, you have been nominated by these instructors for recognition. You have been winners. Recover," stated LT Lyons. He was smiling in a strange way. So, we stood up, confusedly, as our numb feet alone felt the waves push and wash by.

"There is still one event left, as you were briefed, but you seven will not be taking part in it. Boat Crew One, Hell Week is over for you."

Wait, what does that mean? Did we all fail? Where is everyone else? Is this a trick or a joke? What the fuck is going on? we all thought together.

"We need you all to move quietly to the barracks, stow your boat on the boat racks, hang up your kapoks and paddles, wash it all off, and go to bed. Take a shower, eat any stored food you have, but do not leave the barracks. If you see any of your classmates in the other boat crews, do not engage them. They will be told of your accomplishment and reward later. Winning is admired, Gentlemen, and tonight we are all proud to call you winners. There will be some trainees from other classes in the barracks with hot pizza and sodas, and they will take your uniforms to wash and dry them. Congratulations on a job well done. Now go get some sleep. Am I clear?" He then waded into the surf zone and joined us with the other instructors.

A wash of hope and confusion flowed over us. Blood flowed to our heads as one last needed surge of adrenalin was squeezed from within.

Could *this* be it? Was it really over? We had not seen this coming.

They held their hands out as we filed by looking drunk and surprised, and accepted their smiles, shoulder slaps, and congratulations. We were stunned. This was not exactly what we were told to expect. We were being singled out, in a very enjoyable way, but we were not finishing with our class. It was a confusing moment in time, but not for long. It was dark, but dawn did not feel too far away.

We had done it.

"Hooyah," we had responded hoarsely, and with a bit of fear, thinking that this might have been just a trick. But when we all moved towards the barracks and boat racks, no one followed. We were whispering as we moved away cautioning each other to look for a trap, but none appeared.

We stowed our boat, paddles, and kapok lifejackets, washed it all, and walked unbelievingly up the stairs to our second-floor rooms. We were shivering and sandy, and our skin burned where grit and lifejacket straps had rubbed skin raw to the point of bleeding. Blood stained our pants and socks in some cases, and each step noisily squished seawater out of our boots. The adrenalin rush was wearing off, and a deep fatigue was making itself better known.

It seemed more real when we reached the second floor, found a pre-trainee waiting for our clothes, and pointing to some hot pizza standing by for us. We began to partially strip as we walked, leaving a trail of salt, filth, and clothing in the halls or rooms. McNabb had grabbed a piece of pizza, and carried it into the shower with him. He ate it wet. We all walked into the large shower room with twenty shower heads – ten on each side – and turned on every spigot to full hot. The steam began to swirl around us, and we began to shiver more. The heat hit our skin, and it was heavenly. Heat and sleep were our only priority now. Food was less important, as hunger was suppressed by the chemical reactions going on inside us. Our bodies were going to begin a recovery phase, and heat and sleep were most essential.

It was many minutes before we could risk untying our boots, removing our trousers, and bring our macerated, toenail-absent feet out into the warm world. Sand and mud formed rivulets in the water, as it flowed to the floor drains. Tortured feet began to thaw and hurt, and we were moaning and laughing at our suffering. This was a good kind of pain for a change. Circulation was returning to our painful extremities.

Very little was said. Each man was deep within his own foggy thoughts. Sleep was calling and necessary, but our body temperatures were so low now that it was difficult to move, think, or feel warm. Our feet still stung with each step, and the skin above the top of our boots was puffy with thickened, edematous skin that dented in, painfully, when finger tips pushed down, even lightly. The boots came off finally and we noticed our toenails were gone or black. The rush of blood to the now available deep tissue was excruciating. It stung like electric shocks as nutrients attempted to revive dead or dying tissue. Slowly, as some semblance of warmth returned, we ventured under a single shower and adjusted the temperature to hot but tolerable. The hot water heater somewhere must have been very big because the hot water stayed hot for a very long time.

We left all the other showers on full hot, and some just stood in the middle, as steam wafted up and around us. It was like a sublime dream. Our resting hearts were still beating at 120–160 beats per minute, and the warmth rushed to cells in desperate need. We were all depleted of iron and key nutrients, and the brain was confused, both consciously and unconsciously. There was no previous experience for our minds and cellular memories to compare our present state to. It would be unsafe to drive a car, or for that matter sign a legal document. Life was on autopilot, and the autopilot was without direction.

I remember people drifting away from the steaming shower room, and I think we may have said goodbye or goodnight, but I am not sure about that. I do remember being one of the last to leave the hot water, drop my wet clothes by my barracks bed, and climb into the sheets with one Navy issue wool blanket on top. I fell almost instantly asleep. I did not dream. It was about 0300.

At 0400 I awoke with a strange sensation in my bed. It was soaking wet, and so was I. At first, I wondered if I had wet the bed but then noticed that my pillow was wet also. "Did someone throw water on me?"

I felt the wool blanket and it was dry. I was simply covered with sweat. I did not feel hot, but I was sweating heavily. So, I climbed out of bed and went to the shower to rinse off. Seaman McNabb was already there doing the same thing. I told him I woke up covered in sweat, and he noted that the same thing had happened to him. We were not sure what to make of this. It was a bit embarrassing, and then many of the others came in, one by one, to rinse off.

Our core body temperatures had dropped into the high eighties while exposed to chronic wet and cold which, were not for the constant activity and regular feedings, would have resulted in life-threatening hypothermia. Instead, it had reset the hypothalamus in the brain to believe that a lower body temperature was now normal. Thus, when we covered ourselves up, and the autonomic system kicked in, the hypothalamus told our body to get cooler, and the sweating began.

This excessive sleep-sweating would last for months for some. Wives would complain of having to put plastic sheets on their beds. Almost everyone would discover that, for the rest of their lives, they would sweat more than others. This was also true of the heavily frostbitten US Marines who'd survived the Battle of Chosin Reservoir in 1950.

"Many of life's failures are people who did not realize
how close they were to success when they gave up."
—Thomas A. Edison

Chapter 20
Around the World – Saturday pre-dawn Day 6

HOURS WITHOUT SLEEP 116
4 OFFICERS AND 13 ENLISTED
(ONE OFFICER AND SIX ENLISTED ASLEEP IN
THE BARRACKS)

As the winning boat crew was wobbling dazedly to the barracks to find
warmth and sleep. The remaining two boat crews were gathering for a scav-
enger hunt known as Around the World. Feet were swollen to the point
where every footfall felt like bare flesh stomping on hot coals. Necks were
crushed into the shoulders when the IBS was placed on helmets that had
rubbed bald spots on the top of crew cut craniums. Legs were wobbly and
weak; arms were battered, beaten, and covered with crusted over scrapes that
were fighting infections. Brains were numbed and operating on autopilot.

The sky was a tarry, pitch black and without stars. It smelled like rain.
Boat crew leaders were being given the first clue for a trek across the beaches,
bay, or roads to a future map point where another instructor waited to send
them on again and again until sunrise. The boat went with them everywhere.
Their albatross got heavier by the minute.

ENS Albracht was lost in his thoughts, and those thoughts were not very clear. He had relayed the clue to his team, and the consensus was that they were supposed to go to the North Island fence on the north end of the famous Coronado beach, where the rich tourists came for their tans and tubs at the Hotel del Coronado, now lit and visible a few miles away. They were cheating a bit by entering the water to paddle some of the distance to the hotel area. They had been told to walk, but walking caused searing pains for all, so they decided to paddle until close to the lights and then come back in and walk the shorter distance to the fence.

The boat approached stealthily, as crewmen whispered angrily to Randy to "keep the damn boat straight." He, and everyone else, were half asleep now, with their eyes open only by true force of will.

As they reached the invisible beach edge, the surf was calm. A gentle one-foot wave washed them silently onto the surprising beach edge, where they crouched and waited, looking to see if any instructors had viewed their deliberate subterfuge. Everything was quiet, so they began a slow crouched movement up the beach.

Suddenly three vehicles with bright white spotlights came at them from both sides. They froze on the shoreline, silhouetted by the starry sky, and waited for their inevitable punishment for cheating.

A loud speaker from the nearest vehicle blared: "Stand fast and do not move, this is the Coronado Police." That was a surprise, and they froze. The two front men looked at each other and smiled. They then lay down on the black rubber bow and waited. Five seconds later they were fast asleep. They knew that their officers would have to explain this mess, so they rested. It was a welcome break.

ENS Albracht and ENS Johnson raised their hands in surrender, and were motioned forward by the policeman behind the spotlight.

It turned out that some local visitors, who did not know about SEAL training down the beach, had seen the boat full of shady characters, and had assumed the worst. Either they were being invaded from the sea, or more likely, an illicit drug deal was coming ashore. They had called the police, who responded in force immediately.

Neither officer had any identification, other that their names on their helmets, but the police all knew immediately what was going on. Hell Week, and the late night and early morning events associated with it, had scared or confused tourists on a regular basis over the years.

A brief conversation ensued, the lights went off, and the two men were allowed to return to their beached whale of an IBS, where they found the entire crew fast asleep. It had been a glorious ten minutes of rest for them.

They still had a checkpoint to reach, and it was somewhere down the strand. So they wandered toward the only road on the strand, crossed it, and were stumbling under the weight of their boat as they approached the bright exterior lights of the recently closed Chart House restaurant. It was out on a pier, and surrounded by boats tied up in slips, or anchored out in the calm bay water.

It was about 0230, and the crew was moving slowly and deliberately looking for Tom Valentine's car. His wife had been alerted that some time tonight they would be in this area. Tom had called her from the barracks when they had been ordered there to change into dry clothes. She would have food with her, if they could find her.

They did not need to find her. She found them easily. A large rubber boat carried into the lighted restaurant parking lot was rather hard to miss.

"Tom!" she whispered as she and Randy's wife came slowly toward them. They were carrying pizza boxes and bags of peanut butter sandwiches.

Randy was still in a sleep deprived fog when Tom kicked him to focus.

"Huh? Is that them? Where should we go? Did anyone see an instructor?" he mumbled.

Tom pointed to the oyster shell covered dark beach under the piers. "Quick, let's move to the shadows on the beach."

Off they went, with the wives following and looking around conspiratorially.

Two attractive waitresses who had just closed the bar above and stayed for a drink with the bartenders, were leaning over the upper walkway to see the events unfolding below. The movement of black rubber boats with muscular men around Coronado was always worth a pause to observe. When they saw the wives, they giggled and moved on to home.

They all gathered around the boat, and Tom and Randy were rewarded with warm hugs as the pizza boxes flew open and sandwiches were passed around. Cans of Coke popped open, and for a few moments, there was a heavenly silence. Chewing and smacking was all that could be heard. The wives looked on in curiosity and horror. The men all looked like prisoner of war escapees.

The plan had worked, and the crew was rescued as hoped. The food was amazing, and the new flow of calories hit their brains and muscles. A feeling of long lost energy flowed through them, and after a brief thank you hug from each member, the wives disappeared. The quest for their final checkpoint resumed. These two wives would forever be remembered for their much-appreciated rescue mission.

One by one, the two wandering boat crews were directed back to the BUD/S area where a pleased and somewhat respectful group of instructors gathered and planned a movement to their last meal. Logistics were in place as the sun rose for one last well supervised walk across the base to the amphibious base mess hall for one last morning meal. Everyone knew that the sun had come up for the last time. They did not know when the end would come.

"Welcome to Thursday morning, Gentlemen," clapped an instructor. "Only one more day to go."

Confusion washed over many. "Wasn't today Friday? Weren't they close to the end?"

Brains fought to make sense of this cruel joke. The few with more awareness reassured the others, to avoid mutiny, that this was Friday indeed, and the end must be near. The last sunrise had been witnessed, and they were all going to make it.

"Line up your boat crews. Forward march," ordered the now watchful instructors. They knew that this would be a miserable, painful walk, but they were looking at men that now shared knowledge of themselves that only the few here present could know. One day they would likely serve together in war zones yet to be named.

One instructor was starting the van that was filling with instructors and staff. Chief Gosser was in his own car with his wife. They would all go ahead to the mess hall area. The Commander would be there, as would representatives from all three shifts of instructors. This was the event they had all worked towards, and each man still remembered from their own pasts. To be able to relive the moment, with this group, was an honor that only the instructors knew.

The ambulance, with lights flashing for safety, followed the snaking line of two black sandy boats for the long painful march. Grunting, cussing, and moans of anguish could be heard from beneath the coiling rubber procession. Every movement hurt, and every mind was focused on one thing... *the next step.*

One foot in front of the other was all they could focus on now. Food was in the future, and their stomachs were empty again, but the ketone levels from liver and kidney acidosis caused from processing an overload of creatine (a protein breakdown product) from ruptured and destroyed muscle cells had taken away their hunger. They were in a starvation state, and did not know it. This is commonly seen in diabetics when not enough insulin causes a ketoacidosis state, where the body cells, including the brain, get no nutrients. It is quite dangerous.

"Down boats. Line up by boat crew. Leaders report your crews, and set the watch on your boats so we can eat, and get on to the next evolution." came the orders.

By rote, the boats came down softly, with soft cursing and mumbling all around in complaint of the tiniest of irritations.

"Boat crews, right face," and the class turned towards the mess hall entrance.

Quietly, the commander and his crew of instructors moved into formation behind them.

"BUD/S Class 81, about face."

Now, this was unexpected, and as the class stumbled to comply with the order, in some military manner, an American flag unfurled in the morning breeze and the commander stepped forward to announce the end.

There was a moment of confusion and disbelief, followed by a whoop and a holler as helmet liners were thrown in the air in celebration. Hugs and back slapping was the order of the day.

What the commander said, after things calmed down, was lost on all. What happened next, as each instructor stepped forward and shook each survivor's hand, will never be lost. The fog of a last meal and a long painful final walk back to the barracks, followed by the ambulance again, is still difficult to recall.

Not all the men that shared that last meal would go on to graduate. Seventeen finished this first test, but more tests were ahead. There would be academic failures, more injuries, and leadership drops. The search for warrior teammates would continue. Eleven of the men that finished this week would graduate together. Five corpsmen would join us for second and third phase of training and become a permanent part of the class for life.

It rained that day.

"Success is not final, failure is not fatal:
it is the courage to continue that counts."
—Winston S. Churchill

Chapter 21
First phase continues

Hell Week – and the recovery week that followed – marked the middle of the first phase of training. As tadpoles, having completed Hell Week, we had shrunk our tails and grown tiny front legs. We had been physiologically crushed almost to death the week before by muscle fatigue and days of endless, sleeplessness and bleakly low temperatures, while straining to succeed and survive. So, this phase continued gently to give the bodies time to heal. The question of survival was now a distant fear, but many challenges awaited, and the instructors were quick to point that out. Swim times and run times would need to be faster. Academics would get tougher as we learned about diving physiology, weapons operations, demolition characteristics and use, mathematics, first aid, beach reconnaissance, and much more.

0600 PT was mostly stretching and movement of damaged joints and muscles. Toenails needed to re-grow where trench foot had caused them to slough off in wet boots. The severely iron depleted red blood cells needed to be replaced, bringing healing oxygen to muscles and organs that had forgotten what "normal" was. Monday still came on Monday, and training continued. Pool training was emphasized with and without fins.

Later in the following week, the surface dust and grit was blowing towards our beach formation and stung like tiny darts as the phase officer detailed our next task. The four remaining class officers were being briefed by an instructor who was partly drowned out by the wind and surf. Ten-foot crunching waves were beating and slamming themselves against the beach so hard we could feel the concussion through our rubber booties. Our masks and swim fins needed two hands to prevent them from flopping against us. The surf was too dangerous for the safety boats to launch, and so perhaps the frigid two-mile swim event might just be canceled. We hoped so.

"Fall out and gather round," ordered our officer instructor.

"There are no safety boats today, so do not lose sight of your swim buddy," he said with practiced authority.

So much for hope.

"This is not a timed event. Get your fins on at the lifeguard tower. Enter by swim pair at tower. Officers, get your men in the water by squad."

"Sir, is there a recall signal?" I asked respectfully and privately, by walking over to the lieutenant alone. My thoughts were confused. Perhaps this was a test? The December water temperature was 54°F. Our wetsuit tops gave *some* protection and flotation, but I was worried that some swim pairs might not even make it out through the surf. We were talking officer-to-officer. But my only rank display was ENS stenciled on my helmet. His two silver bars seemed to sparkle as bits of the beach sand bounced by. His voice softened a bit.

"No recall signal and no safety boats due to the surf. This is an easy non-timed event to help your bodies recover and stay in shape. Get your team in the water, sir."

I paused, still concerned and hoping for "April fools," but when no other option presented, I snapped to a tighter attention.

"Yes sir," I said with doubt in my voice.

Nearby, on the cement walk from Ocean Boulevard to the lifeguard tower, stood six curious onlookers. We were alone on the stormy beach, and they had either wandered over from the Hotel del Coronado or had come from the extremely expensive homes that lined the boulevard facing us. They were bundled against the weather, but not moving until the drama on the beach unfolded.

"Guys, listen up. Don and I will go first as we are the strongest swimmers. If we get out through the breakers, follow quickly, but stay together. Hold hands if you need to."

I was sure this was going to be very difficult for all.

I had to say something more. This was my class now.

"They did not brief this, but look or listen for a recall signal. If it is bad out there they will likely call us back. So, let's go." I saw nods all around.

"On me and Don." I ordered. "Be safe."

And with that we all moved towards the deafening roar of waves crashing ahead.

I bent to put on my fins, popped my mask in place, tightened the UDT grey life vest straps, and felt for my K-bar knife. It hung off my life vest strapped on the right side. Olive drab duct tape held my MK-13 smoke/flare tightly to the gray plastic knife sheath. I was ready.

"OK Donnie, let's do it."

We both waddled backwards toward the waves pounding toward us. The first wave hit my calf with an icy arctic blast of white foam. I was holding Don's hand tightly as we stumbled carefully through the pushing, pulling, and sucking Pacific surf.

Two feet deep, and our testicles automatically tucked up higher as icy fingers seized our legs and groins. We were both very grateful for the flap of wetsuit rubber that wrapped tightly between our legs. The next wave hit me from behind as the returning water rolled under one of my front fins. Suddenly, I was underwater and pulling Don down with me. He tried to lift me out of the chaos to no avail. So, we both started to swim together with fins kicking through the froth and hitting the rock-hard bottom simultaneously. We rolled to our sides and began side stroking through the now monstrous waves, holding on was impossible with numb hands.

A ten-foot wave has a ten-foot peak and a ten-foot trough. The result is a twenty-foot rise from trough to peak, and we were now human-powered corks. There was a strong inshore current working against us. With both of us swimming hard and gasping for air as breaking waves slammed over us without warning, I was swallowing salt water involuntarily, to avoid choking when I looked up to find Don. He had the same issue, but since he was upwind and up-current from me, he was getting it worse than I was – that first blast of wind and water.

I puked. Breakfast came back up mixed with salt water and stomach acid. Not a lot, but it burned, and it reminded me of the huge portion of bacon, eggs, and cheese, with three large Pepsi's I had engulfed for breakfast recently. I wondered briefly if sharks were attracted to bacon, eggs, and cheese.

We were going nowhere fast. There was no chance we were going to complete two miles today. But we were going to try. I could still see the lifeguard tower on shore aligned with us. We had made no progress in over twenty minutes of swimming.

Randy and Rosy were hundreds of yards back from our launch point. The inshore current was much stronger than anyone had expected. Both swimmers were still trying to learn how to use the World War II era UDT Duck Foot fins we had been issued. They were light brown, thick, and heavy. Randy had never used fins in his life before BUD/S. He enjoyed swimming in the Missouri river back home, but as a wrestler, with not a hint of body fat to start, he lacked some of the natural floatation and insulation that fat provided. Rosy had lost the last of his baby fat finally. They both now looked like poster models for SEAL recruiting ads.

Rosy shouted to Randy, "This current is too strong. We need to get farther out to sea, I think."

"Worth a try," Randy responded encouragingly, but out of breath.

Fins were still not his best friend. Both needed some encouragement, as they knew this was going to be one more test for both. Randy had failed to pass both fin swims in first phase so far, due to leg cramps while learning to use fins. He had been brought before a retention board where he had been given a final chance. Pass the swim test or find another profession. Rosy was his swim buddy because he had also failed to pass the one-mile swim. Rosy and Randy had been practicing side stroke and breast stroke with fins in the NAB pool during first phase. This was their chance to prove what they had learned. So, they changed the angle of their swim to 45 degrees out to sea. One hour later they were finally making progress. Two hours later, a Coast Guard helicopter flew by over the inshore waves, low and fast, in the stormy weather.

They both thought the same thing: *I wonder what they are doing out here in this weather?*

"I think I saw a flare," Don shouted through the surf and wind noise. I looked toward the tower at the beach launch point. We both slowed our swim pace, and then we both saw it. Someone was throwing a MK-13 flare in the air.

"Hooyah."

We were slowing our swim pace now as we worked our way back in to the beach. A few swim pairs were already assembled at the tower. They had either not made it out at all, or had washed up further down from our starting point.

One by one, the swim pairs straggled back to the starting point, and stood there shivering in the wind, as we counted heads. One pair was unaccounted for. Randy and Rosy were our weakest swimmers, and we all knew that they had not yet passed their one-mile timed swim. They had been allowed to go on anyway, but had been warned that they would need to pass soon or face bring dropped. They were nowhere in sight.

We were thinking the worst. Or weighing its possibility at the very least. *Randy and Rosy drowned?*

The instructors ordered us to move down-current along the beach towards the North Island rock jetty looking for them (or their bodies).

"Surely, they would have inflated their life jackets?"

It was time for another semi-respectful chat with the lieutenant.

"Sir, the class is out looking. I hope you realize that both these men are married. If I must speak to their wives tonight, you and I are going to have another very unpleasant conversation."

His eyes widened a bit, and I knew he saw what I meant. The choices he had made today would put his career at risk. He nodded and turned away to do what needed to be done, if rescue was possible.

Back at the BUD/S area, a truck slid into the front lot, and the driver sprinted to the commander's office. Things happened fast after that. Coast Guard Air Sea Rescue was notified, and helicopters were launched to search the area. Instructors hopped in cars and came to help look. Others stayed along the sand berms, behind the training area and quietly hoped for the best. A few prayed. I paced back and forth along our search area and worried that I would not see Randy or Rosy again. I was angry at that possibility.

Time dragged on, and hope for the best was getting difficult.

Five and a half hours after the recall signal was thrown into the air, they were found. Randy and Rosy, exhausted and almost hypothermic from exposure, crawled out of the surf zone at the designated finish point. They were very proud of themselves. They had accomplished the improbable, and had no idea if they were first or last. The only thing they had been sure of was that they were not going to quit. An instructor standing on the berm had already learned that these were the worst fin swimmers in the class and was sure that *someone's* career was over. He had to look twice, and then again, before he realized what he saw. Everyone else was looking north where the bodies would likely be found. He had the quarterdeck watch and could not leave, so there he stood, watching the wind and waves when they straggled in.

"Holy shit!" he hooted as he ran down the berm to help. "Are you our missing swimmers?!"

Confused but immensely proud of what they knew they had accomplished, they looked at each other then back at the man.

"Hooyah, Instructor. I guess we were last in again, huh?"

"Well Gents, you sure did scare the crap out of a lot of men today, but I think you will be pleased to learn that, as the *only* finishers of the swim, you win. And most likely, you just passed your first phase swim test."

About that same time, two other instructors came over to see what was going on at the beach. They were almost in awe now, after assuming the worst. They ran down to help and literally picked up the two swimmers with rock hard, cold, unfeeling legs and carried them up the sandy dunes to the grinder where they were directed to the first phase officer's office. The coffee was hot, and a small crowd gathered to hear their story again, and again.

ENS Randy Albracht went on to serve thirty years with the Teams retiring as a Captain (SEAL), and Rosy Rosensweig, after completing our Hell Week was rolled back to the later Class 82, due to slower run times, and he would finish with that class. He served twenty-two years, and retired as a Chief Petty Officer (SEAL) respected by all who would serve with him.

"You measure the size of the accomplishment by the obstacles you had to overcome to reach your goals."
—Booker T. Washington

Chapter 22
Graduation

Of the seventeen who had survived Hell week, eleven graduated Class 81. Injuries, failed standards, and academics had lessened the final graduation number. There were also five corpsmen that joined us after Hell Week, to go through the diving and land warfare phases. They would always be part of our class, but the Navy *needed* corpsmen, so Hell Week was bypassed to increase graduation rates for those necessary teammates.

We were all in dress blue uniforms to accept our graduation certificates. The Xeroxed graduation certificates we were awarded were thin pieces of paper, with a gold seal, and blue and gold ribbons applied to the right lower corner, titled:

Naval Technical Training Command
Certificate of Graduation
"(Typed name here)"
Has successfully completed the prescribed course of instruction in
Basic Underwater Demolition/SEAL Training
Dated 4 April 1975

The chairs were few. The crowd was invited and *small*.

A speech was made and forgotten, but the event was memorialized by a photograph with eleven men gathered out front of the training area with Seaman Robert McNabb holding the Honor Man certificate. Three officers and eight enlisted men gathered for a photo that would be displayed at the Fort Pierce, Florida SEAL museum alongside all the past and future SEAL classes.

The Honor Man is a special award given to one man in each graduating class. The qualifications to earn this special recognition from the cadre of instructors are not published.

There was a discussion and serious debate by the instructors to determine who best exemplified the Teams and would continue to serve with honor. Bob McNabb would prove them right, in combat and in peacetime, for decades to follow.

This was a moment in all our lives that would live forever in our collective memories. It was accented by the handshakes of the veterans that welcomed us to the fraternity we were now a part of. We were no longer tadpoles. We were frogmen.

Our five medical classmates were missing from the photo. All our corpsmen were present, but not considered for the graduation photo since they had been treated as non-combatants by the Navy at that time, and not required to do Hell Week. The potential training loss rate would be unacceptably high for these men with special and needed skills.

One of these corpsmen would later join the police force and earn two medals of valor under fire, and one other would later serve a brilliant career in the CIA.

The Teams would always honor their corpsmen, and the future would find changes in policy allowing corpsmen to train more completely for combat and be tested by Hell Week. One corpsman, Senior Chief Edward Byers would be awarded the Team's sixth SEAL Medal of Honor, in 2016, for his actions in Afghanistan. His team would rescue a Taliban-captured American doctor, lose one teammate in the rescue, and see this medical trained operator use both his combat and medical skills to the benefit of America and his teammates.

After accepting the long sought-after diplomas, which acknowledged that Class 81 had made it, we all moved down the line of instructors and leaders that were welcoming us into the Teams. We then each walked to the potentially ignominious brass bell, and rang it loudly and ceremoniously three times. The bell no longer represented a threat. It signaled, for all to hear – *success*.

To this day, despite many other momentous events in our lives, most of us will recall with pride, the handshakes that we were offered by our instructors. Chief Rogers reserved the personal privilege, and right, to render a first Team salute to the three officers that had finished with our class. Steve Frisk, who would train, and see, nineteen classes graduate, and had guided us all, shook our hands and smiled with pride. Mike Thornton, wearing a dress uniform adorned with the Medal of Honor ribbon, smiled like a new dad. We were his first class to train.

"Welcome to the Teams, sir," Chief Rogers stated as he whipped a perfect salute to each officer individually. This moment would resonate in our individual and collective memories as the ultimate recognition of our personal achievements to date.

The chief petty officer that had accosted and challenged the eight officers in our class to prove to him that we could lead his teammates into combat, rendered our first salute at graduation to only three, as new members of his elite community. We would each go on to earn other salutes and awards, but none would be more memorable than *that* one, respectfully rendered, which he honored us with that day.

As for me personally, I cannot recall a more satisfying life moment.

Afterword

"When a man finds that it is his destiny to suffer, he will have to accept his suffering as his task; his single and unique task. He will have to acknowledge the fact that even in suffering he is unique and alone in the universe. No one can relieve him of his suffering or suffer in his place. His unique opportunity lies in the way in which he bears his burden."

—Dr. Viktor Frankle, *Man's Search for Meaning*.

The persons in this book and their stories are real. I chose to emphasize certain common experiences and personal characteristics that I have learned to appreciate over the many years spent trying to understand why some men finish Hell Week while others do not.

As a physician, I treat life stresses as often as I treat most other diseases. I feel qualified to comment on the learning gleaned from decades serving patients dealing with stress and apply that experience to the story.

There is not an uncomplicated way to tell you what it takes to *be a winner*. In my opinion, every man who completes training, graduates, and is accepted into the special operations community will be a better person for the experience.

Clearly, as Mike Suter and Frank Winget demonstrated, having tried and failed the first time is a great motivator for success a second time, but in both cases, there were previous life challenging experiences that added greatly to their chances of success.

Every man that goes to BUD/S swears to himself, and others, that he will never quit. Each event in every day is designed to challenge that promise. Faith in one's self cannot be allowed to waiver. The end of Hell Week is a defined point, but each challenge offered and met must be viewed as just one step towards that end.

To allow one's self to measure the time until it ends is to invite doubt. When you doubt if you can stay in the chilly water one more second, or doubt your ability to run one more step, you must reach inside and pull the faith in yourself back to the present. Faith in one more step, faith in one more minute of cold endurance, and faith that the end will come when it comes. This will permit you to be there with the others. If the man next to you can endure, so can you.

Two of our starting class officers, would try again and fail again. When faced with the brutality of their situations, they would lose faith in themselves a second time. I suspect it was in part due to their previous life successes. They had not yet failed enough, or been tested enough by life's many available hard events and surprises. They allowed themselves to think ahead. The distance to the finish line was too far away. They had other places that they could go and still feel good about those options. Most (if not all) of the graduates that this story was about, had no place else they were willing to go.

That is what they knew in their hearts, what they felt deep in their bones, and was engraved in their souls.

"I have seen worse. I can and *will* go on."

Their unwillingness to accept any option other than staying the course to the end – and their ability to embrace the essential concept that the only easy day was yesterday – proved to be their learned life blessing and their salvation.

Those that have endured life's many challenges, and who have incorporated those successes as part of themselves, will succeed in later endeavors. The lessons of this narrative apply to all persons in every walk of life. Endure, and survive the challenges that life throws at you (especially those that you cannot control), and the future will be yours to control.

In all the years that I have shared the stories of the men I trained with, I have never admitted to others that I was disappointed that I never actually discovered my personal limit. I was told to expect it. I wanted to find it, so I could move past it, but I had more to give. I have felt guilty that perhaps I was not as good as I was supposed to be, by failing to *almost* fail. When my Hell Week ended, I was grateful and exhausted, but I could have gone further.

I realized by telling this story – and listening to the others – that I was not the only one that did not discover their physical or mental end points before the week ended. I suggest now, in retrospect, that it was because life had already shown a more difficult distant end-point to us. Others, like me, had already had the "shit kicked out of us" so many times already, that the *limit* we would need to find in Hell Week was beyond what the instructors could imagine, or *even legally require.*

Yet by completing Hell Week, we could acknowledge our already life-learned lessons as immensely valuable. Our success was highly likely from the start. We had already, in our previous experiences, stepped over the invisible line that few are willing to acknowledge or talk about.

To choose a future frogman, or business leader to function in a challenging environment, it is likely that past life challenges will prove to be the best distinguishing factor.

Epilogue

Many have faced the indescribable moment, when absolutely everything that they hold dear hangs in the balance. Those who completed Hell Week discovered much about themselves that most will never learn, or need to know. They discovered what very few can. That the perceived impossible is possible.

All eleven men, plus the five corpsmen, who graduated with Class 81 went on to successful careers and lives. Most of the men highlighted in this narrative stayed in the military for a career, and are all still enjoying, or did enjoy, a life of success. Every enlisted sailor that remained, was commissioned, and progressed in rank as an officer or warrant officer.

Their brotherhood remains close today.

BUDS/Class 81

ENS Robert Adams – CDR (SEAL), COL USA	UDT-11, NSWG-1, Navy Parachute Team, ST-4 Reserve, DELTA Force (Army), 82nd Airborne Iraq (Army)
ENS Randy Albracht -- CAPT (SEAL)	UDT-12, ST-1, BUD/S Instructor, ST-2 Reserve, SOCKorea, Allied Forces Iraq, SOC JFCOM(Res)
ENS John Muggs (pseudonym) – LCDR (SEAL)	Numerous classified NSW commands
PN2 Mike Suter – CW5 (SEAL), (deceased)	Numerous classified NSW commands
RM2 Tom Valentine – LCDR (SEAL)	ST-1, Navy Parachute Team, ST-3, AmphibGRU-2, classified NSW commands, BUPERS
FTG3 Frank Winget – CAPT (SEAL)	UDT-21, ST-2 Reserve, NSWG-4 Res, USSOCOM
SA Bob McNabb – LCDR (SEAL)	UDT -11, UDT-21, numerous classified NSW commands
SA Don Sayre – CDR (SEAL)	UDT-21, SDV-2, Special Boat Unit 20, ST-2, NSWG-2, classified NSW command, C.O. ST-8
MM3 David Banton	UDT 12, ST-1, Navy Parachute Team
ATAN Tom Hanrath	UDT-21, ST-1
SA David Hyman – (deceased)	ST-1
HM3 Greg Kelly – corpsman	
HM3 Ronald Relf – corpsman	
HM3 Richard Schott – corpsman	
HM3 James Shoemate – corpsman	
HM3 Steven Shrunk – corpsman	

About The Author

Colonel Robert Adams, MD, MBA served fourteen years in the Navy and eighteen years in the Army. He changed services to attend medical school, and applies his analytical skill to look back at the men that shivered and struggled through Hell Week together. He brings decades of insight learned caring for others to an insightful analysis of why the men of his BUD/S class 81 achieved the improbable.

CPSIA information can be obtained
at www.ICGtesting.com
Printed in the USA
BVOW03s1332141217

502801BV00001B/28/P